a collection
of **simple,
stylish
& spirited**
knits

the
best
of

knitscene

lisa shroyer

INTERWEAVE.
interweave.com

EDITOR
Ann Budd

PHOTOGRAPHER
Joe Hancock, unless otherwise noted

PHOTO STYLIST
Carol Beaver

HAIR + MAKEUP
Kathy MacKay

COVER + INTERIOR DESIGN
Pamela Norman

ILLUSTRATION
Gayle Ford, unless otherwise noted

PRODUCTION
Katherine Jackson

Interweave Press LLC
201 East Fourth Street
Loveland, CO 80537
interweave.com

Printed in China by C&C Offset

Library of Congress Cataloging-
in-Publication Data
Shroyer, Lisa.
The Best of Knitscene: a collection
of simple, stylish, and spirited knits /
Lisa Shroyer.
p. cm.
Includes bibliographical references
and index.
ISBN 978-1-59668-326-6 (pbk.)
ISBN 978-1-59668-888-9 (eBook)
1. Knitting. I. Knitscene. II. Title.
TT820.S5225 2011
746.43'2--dc23
2011012151

10 9 8 7 6 5 4 3 2 1

acknowledgments

A big THANKS is owed to the designers and writers who have contributed to *Knitscene*'s success. You guys keep us all knitting!

And thanks to all former editors of *Knitscene*: Pam Allen, Clara Parkes, and Katie Himmelberg.

Because patterns are the core of the publication, I cannot say "thank you" enough to the technical editors who have worked on the magazine, and therefore this book. You really keep us all knitting.

And lastly, thanks to Marilyn Murphy, who took a chance on an assistant editor when she let me try my hand at directing a magazine. That chance has made all the difference.

contents

welcome to the 'scene

Simple, stylish knitting for the free spirit; this is the *Knitscene* mission. From its debut in 2005 as a special issue to its progression to quarterly status in 2011, we have sought out fresh projects, up-and-coming designers, unusual yarns, and fun ways to photograph them. This anthology celebrates the best of those efforts from the magazine's first five years.

I was lucky enough to work on the very first issue with then-editor Pam Allen—I had just started working at Interweave—and to now have served as editor of the title for eight issues (with more on the way!). I've chosen these twenty projects for three key reasons: their unique approach to design; their reflection of the *Knitscene* mission of simple, stylish knitting; and their popularity with real knitters—these projects rate very highly on sites such as KnittingDaily.com and Ravelry.com.

To bring everything up to date, we've redone the photography and tweaked some of the original designs to eliminate discontinued yarns and colors. This book takes content, originally time-sensitive in the magazine format, and presents it in a classic way that will appeal for years to come.

I hope you enjoy these old favorites and the many new looks to come from *Knitscene*.

Lisa Shroyer
Editor, *Knitscene*

From the *runway* to *Knitscene* to *real* knitters—*trends* in knitwear

by **KATE SONNICK**

I DON'T KNOW about you, but whenever I spy a super-chic knitwear design in a fashion magazine, my first thought is, I could knit that. I've fondled $3,000 cable-knit handbags in Bergdorf's while muttering to myself, *I could knit that*. My favorite fashion blogs gush over slouchy berets and chunky snoods, and I smile to myself and say, *I could knit those*. I've drooled over the pom-pommed thigh-highs at Alexander Mc-Queen, the braided headbands at Prada, the punk-rock fishnets at Rodarte, and the oversized boyfriend sweaters at Stella McCartney. Guess what, guys? *I could knit those.*

I won't deny that knitting is about utility and craft and yarny, tactile goodness. But more than that, it's a way to rock the latest runway looks without having to drain my bank account. It's a way to be creative. To express my personal style. And even if I don't end up knitting those couture master-pieces, I'm endlessly amazed and inspired by them.

The great thing about *Knitscene* is that you can find the ele-ments of style on every page. With designs that are as fashion-forward as they are fast and simple to knit. And, to my mind, the best part of *Knitscene* is that so many of the designs can be easily adapted and styled to reflect the latest fashion trend.

To show you what I mean, let's take a look at three design techniques. While each is part of a time-honored handknit tradition, each has also been a fixture on the catwalks over the past few seasons. Not to mention an integral part of an enlightened ensemble on celebrities and trendsetters from Soho to Hollywood.

Want to know where these tech-niques came from, what gives them their sartorial staying power, and how to style them in a fresh way? The knitwear designs that emerge from each of these timeless techniques are just the beginning. Because it's not just what or how you knit, it's how you wear what you knit to express your unique style. I hope you'll be inspired to cast on more than one of these *Best of Knitscene* designs. And while you're at it, to create a truly of-the-moment look that becomes a "Best Of" in your own wardrobe. Just don't be surprised if you hear one of your BFFs mumbling, *I could knit that.*

real knitters

1. Jacqueline Tung worked the **Indigo Banded Cardigan** (*Knitscene*, Fall 2009) with a close fit for a femme take on the Cowichan archetype. **2.** Knitter Ali Farris designed her own Cowichan-styled sweater. Try charting large animal motifs and inserting them into your next project to get the same look.
3. Lacey Holbert knit just the colorwork cowl of the **Ninebark Cowl** (*Knitscene*, Winter/Spring 2010). The stripes of simple color patterns are easy for a Fair Isle newbie. **4.** Knitter AZURE shows how rustic cables fit an urban sensibility with the **Heather Hoodie Vest** (see page 90). **5.** Paulina Wisniewska inserted a zipper in the **Central Park Hoodie** (see page 20) to give this cabled classic a true sportswear feel. **6.** Melissa Mulder's tweedy **Central Park Hoodie** (see page 20) shows off rope cables beautifully.

cowichan

①

what it is

Let me make one thing perfectly clear. The term "Cowichan" is reserved for sweaters handknitted by native Canadian Northwest Coast Salish tribes. Everything else is just a Cowichan wannabe. But you can't blame a cardigan for wishing it were one of these works of folk art.

The Canadian winter style staple is as charmingly ironic as it is stylishly iconic. Katherine Hepburn cozied up in one. It was the star of *Starsky & Hutch*. And, The Dude from *The Big Lebowski* abided in one.

Genuine Cowichan sweaters are knitted from undyed, handspun wool and boast patterns inspired by Western Canada's flora and fauna. Authentic designs are still being produced in limited quantities today. But, knitter beware: just because a sweater has a deer or snowflake motif doesn't mean it's the real McCoy. Check for a label that says it's handknit by members of the Cowichan tribe.

TODD NAKASHIMA

why we love it

It doesn't hurt that it's been hyped by fashion bloggers and spotted on Hollywood celebrities. The Canadian fashion label Granted (www.grantedclothing.com) has created a quirky riff on the faux-Co style, subbing palm trees for pines and camels for grizzly bears. And high-end designers from Twinkle's Wenlan Chia to Ralph Lauren have sent inspired styles down the runway more than once.

Knitscene designer Courtney Kelley also pays homage to the style in her book, *Vintage Modern Knits*. "In times of economic uncertainty, it follows that people would turn to garments that evoke home, handmade, tradition, warmth, and comfort," she says. As much as Courtney appreciates traditional design elements, she also likes to add her own modern touches, such as unexpected colors and a body-conscious fit.

As for the style's enduring appeal, Courtney says it's all about fashion's cyclical nature. She points out that Cowichan's folk elements had a moment in the early 1990s grunge movement. "Think lumberjacks, flannel shirts, *Twin Peaks*," she says. Now it's back—but with "a more refined style of folksy . . . and a certain fashion irony."

make it your own BFF

A sort of über-grandpa cardigan, your own Cowichan-inspired sweater can be a great foil for slim silhouettes, bold patterns, and sparkly fabrics. *Knitscene* designer Cecily Glowik MacDonald's Indigo Banded Cardigan is a simple way to feel the Cowichan love with its creamy white base and midriff band of colorwork. Follow Hollywood star Megan Fox's lead and throw it on over a slouchy white V-neck T-shirt. Add a pair of metal aviators and silky cargoes for a comfy travel look. Pair it with a vintage-y plaid blouse, skinny jeans, and tall boots. Wrap yourself up in one over a sequin tank dress for an offbeat glam effect.

1. A *Knitscene* classic: **The Indigo Banded Cardigan** by Cecily Glowik MacDonald appeared in *Knitscene* Fall 2009. With its shawl collar, white main color, and foreground colorwork in a solid navy, this simple cardi evokes Cowichan style while not mimicking any archetype. (This pattern is available for individual sale at interweavestore.com.) **2.** Modern interpretation: Courtney Kelley plays with the Cowichan type in the **Maple Bay Cardigan** from *Vintage Modern Knits* (Interweave, 2011).

fair isle

what it is

I can close my eyes and see a portrait of the Prince of Wales, circa 1921. The image is etched in my mind, but not because he's holding a terrier who looks just like my dog, Mac. It's because, along with a jaunty cap, he's sporting what must be the quintessential Fair Isle pullover.

Fair Isle knitting takes its name from a wee little island off the coast of Scotland. Loosely defined, it refers to any type of banded colorwork. In its strictest form, Fair Isle is knitted in the round, with no more than two colors across a single row, to create small, repetitive, geometric motifs. Whether you're a purist or laid back in your knitterly views, I think we can all say aye on one thing: Fair Isle is most excellent.

why we love it

Images of the handsome Prince in the pullover set off a frenzy for Fair Isle style back in the 1920s. Flash forward about ninety years: Victoria Beckham set paparazzi bulbs ablaze when she stepped out in a jaunty cap, skinny jeans, and an Alexander McQueen Fair Isle pullover.

Along with traditional geometric shapes, McQueen's version rocked a band of skulls. Now that's what we call posh spice.

Marc Jacobs also has a fever for the Fairest. Jacobs' Fall 2010 showstopper, knit up in neutral hues, was paired with a similarly hued, below-the-knee, graphic print skirt and slouchy anklets worn with heels. The look was at once traditional and modern; it made me want to reach into the black hole in the back of my closet to see if I could dig out any of the Fair Isle ski sweaters my Mom wore in the 1960s.

And Jacobs isn't the only designer to channel his inner snow bunny. Dolce & Gabbana had a sexy "Look, Ma, no pants!" take on the trend you're not likely to find in your mother's closet anytime soon.

1. The **Road to Golden Pullover** appeared in *Knitscene* Fall 2007. With its horizontal bands of colorwork, it references traditional Fair Isle knitting, but a worsted-weight yarn and sections of solid-color stockinette are totally contemporary. This pattern is available for sale at interweavestore.com. **2.** The **Prince of Wales** first popularized the Fair Isle jumper in the 1920s (courtesy of Shetland Museum and Archives). **3.** Allover peerie patterns and star motifs are common in Scandinavian colorwork traditions. *Photo by Joe Coca.* **4.** The **Ninebark Cowl** from *Knitscene* Winter/Spring 2010. This pattern is available in the Winter/Spring 2010 digital edition at interweavestore.com. The stripes of simple color patterns are easy for a newbie.

Knitscene designer Elinor Brown thinks Fair Isle has such enduring appeal "because no matter how it's made—yarn, colors, stitch patterns—what's old is made new again." She says stranded colorwork offers more room to play. "The stockinette sweater has been knitted and re-knitted a million times over." With Fair Isle, you get to change the color palette or the charted pattern. "And suddenly you have an entirely different look from the same written pattern. I love how ten versions of a stranded pattern can look like they came from ten different patterns."

make it your own BFF

Fair Isle sweater style is as easy as throwing one on over a pair of jeans and boots. *Knitscene*'s popular Ninebark Cowl, designed by the Berrocco Design Team, would lend a classic camel coat some folkloric charm. But why stop there? Take a cue from D&G and infuse a traditional, fitted Fair Isle pullover with a dose of up-to-the-minute sass: a pair of satiny shorts and lace-up booties. Or make your Marc in a Fair Isle sweater teamed with a contrasting print skirt.

JOE COCA

cables

what it is

You may wish upon a star, but have you ever wished upon a cable? In the early 1900s, the intricate braids on an Aran sweater were said to be a wish for luck and safety to the Irish fisherman who wore the fabled cables to sea.

And if you think that's romantic, consider this: each Aran design was said to be unique to a given family. The reason? To help identify the body of said fisherman if he were to become not so lucky. Turns out that story is a myth. Or perhaps a clever marketing ploy by the early proponents of the craft. Either way, by the 1940s, demand for the richly cabled Irish sweaters boomed. And it shows no sign of busting.

why we love it

Speaking of busts, while on a USO tour in 1952, Marilyn Monroe was asked what she thought about sweater girls. She replied, "Not much. I mean, take away their sweaters and what have they got?" Of course, Marilyn would know. She famously shimmied in a cable sweater and little else in the 1960 film *Let's Make Love.*

The fashion world is full of scanty, filmy, wispy, and risqué. So it's a relief to see cable knits you can cozy up in while you're, say, standing next to an iceberg as the models did at a recent Chanel show. And Prada recently put chunky knit cables on everything from knee socks to skirts to headbands.

Whether high fashion or high function, it's hard to deny the textural appeal of the sculptural peaks and valleys of handknit cables. Just ask Heather Lodinsky, the mastermind of our most sought-after *Knitscene* design: the Central Park Hoodie, shown above (and on page

20). At last count, nearly 6,000 knitters on Ravelry.com had it queued. It even has its own acronym, CPH.

"Cables are fascinating," Heather says. "I can remember when I was young, seeing a cable cardigan that my mom had knitted, and I could only imagine that she had actually cut her knitting to make those cables!" Heather later found cables weren't nearly as complicated as she had originally envisioned. And she set out to prove it to knitters worldwide, many of whom claim the beloved CPH as their very first cable knit project.

make it your own BFF

Heather says she's oohed and ahhed over the myriad modifications knitters have made to her original design. If I were making the CPH right now, I'd consider turning it into a hooded sweater dress, a chic riff on recent runway looks. Whether it's the CPH or another cable knit sweater design, a great way to style it is to throw on a skinny belt in a bright color, a la Prada. For a decidedly downtown vibe, pair an oversized chunky cable pullover with leather shorts and tights. Or create a polished look for the office, pulling a cropped cable sweater over a pair of high-waisted trousers and finishing the look with ladylike pumps.

KATE SONNICK is an advertising copywriter, fashion blogger, and knitter in upstate New York. She has been penning the *Knitscene* Stylespotting column since 2008. Taking the very last page in every issue, this beloved department owes its longevity to Kate's witty take on fashion knitting. You can find more of her style and wit at knitlit.blogspot.com.

1. Crossed stitches can be combined with ribbing, bobbles, and other stitches for a fisherman look or used singularly for a more contemporary style. *Photo by Joe Coca.*
2 + 3. The **Central Park Hoodie** by Heather Lodinsky and **Heather Hoodie Vest** by Debbie O'Neill. Patterns found on pages 20 and 90.

the weighty world of *yarn*

by **CLARA PARKES**

Knitting has its own lingo. Not only do we speak in acronyms ("My WIP is an FO!"), but we use odd and somewhat archaic terms such as worsted, fingering, and DK to describe yarn types. They refer to the weight, or thickness, of a yarn, which determines its gauge and ideal applications. Let's walk through all the yarn weights, from the cobweb-thin to the big and bulky, and translate them into terms you can remember the next time you're at your local yarn store.

What follows are approximations and averages based on an imaginary world where everything is knitted in perfect squares of cohesive stockinette. But we don't always knit this way. Sometimes we knit lace patterns out of yarns that aren't laceweight. Sometimes we knit socks out of yarns that are thicker or finer than traditional sock-weight yarns. Sometimes we may knit an item out of three strands of superfine yarn that, when knit together, produce an entirely different gauge. The weights simply create a general framework; the exceptions are yours to discover.

We start with the finest of the fine, those yarns that could double as sewing thread or dental floss—almost. You'll see them called *superfine, fingering, baby, laceweight, cobweb*, or *sock*. Technically this weight of yarn is reserved for lace, socks, heirloom baby items, or perhaps an intricate colorwork pair of mittens or a hat. When knitting a standard stockinette fabric from this weight of yarn, you'd use U.S. size 1 to 3 (2.25 to 3.25 mm) needles at a gauge of 27 to 32 stitches per 4" (10 cm). But many times you'll use superfine yarns for openwork lace that's knit on much larger needles. It'll look strange and jumbled as you work, but when you finish and wash the lace, you'll be able to expand it to almost twice its size.

Next up we have *fine* and *sportweight* yarns. These yarns are fine enough for socks, mittens, some lace, and delicate baby clothes, but they're also suitable for lightweight sweaters. Fine/sportweight yarns knit up at 23 to 26 stitches per 4" (10 cm) on U.S. size 3 to 5 (3.25 to 3.75 mm) needles.

Moving along in the thickness scale, we reach a transitional category of yarns that aren't fine enough to be sportweight but are slightly finer than the next category. These yarns go by the terms **DK** (which stands for **double-knitting**) or **light worsted** and tend to knit up at 21 to 24 stitches per 4" (10 cm) on U.S. size 5 to 7 (3.75 to 4.5 mm) needles.

Our next category, **worsted-weight** or **medium-weight yarn**, is a favorite general-purpose yarn weight for all sorts of projects. It's also the source of some confusion because the term worsted has two very different definitions, depending on its context. In terms of yarn weight, worsted or medium yarn knits up at 16 to 20 stitches per 4" (10 cm) on U.S. size 7 to 9 (4.5 to 5.5 mm) needles.

But in terms of yarn itself, the term worsted also refers to any yarn—regardless of weight—whose fibers have been combed and closely aligned prior to spinning. Worsted-spun yarns tend to be smooth and lustrous, with excellent stitch definition. On the other end of the spectrum we have woolen-spun yarns, whose fibers stay jumbled prior to spinning. Woolen-spun yarns tend to produce a loftier, fuzzier fabric with a greater variety of needle sizes—the yarn simply expands or contracts to fill whatever space you give it.

Now we reach those bulkier instant-gratification yarns that let you knit up an entire sweater in one weekend. Termed **bulky** or **chunky**, and sometimes

referred to as **rug yarns**, these thick yarns knit up at a speedy 12 to 15 stitches per 4" (10 cm) on U.S. size 9 to 11 (5.5 to 8 mm) needles. Bulky or chunky yarns are great for quick-knitting items of all sorts—scarves, hats, bags, and even sweaters. But keep in mind that these yarns produce a bulky fabric with extremely obvious stitches. Lace, cables, and other patterned stitches tend to get blown out of proportion in bulky yarns, although some designers use this effect to their advantage.

And finally, we reach the bulkiest of the **bulky, super bulky** or **super chunky**, also sometimes referred to as **polar** or **roving**. These yarns are best suited for bulky outerwear, such as jackets and

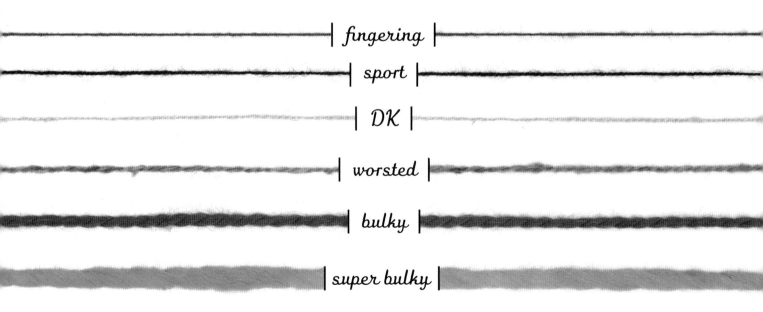

fingering

sport

DK

worsted

bulky

super bulky

> yarns with natural fibers weigh less or more depending on the amount of moisture in the environment, since those fibers readily absorb whatever ambient moisture is in the air.

coats, although you can also use them for quick-knitting afghans and scarves. Super-bulky yarns knit up at 6 to 11 stitches per 4" (10 cm) on needles ranging from U.S. size 11 (8 mm) to baseball bats and beyond.

You'll notice that I often used the word "weight" in conjunction with these terms—worsted weight, medium weight, fingering weight, etc. Today, when we talk about a yarn in terms of weight, we're often referring to its thickness. This odd word use harks back to the days when patterns specified yarn requirements in terms of weight rather than yards, and when most skeins weighed the same. But that approach didn't take into account the fiber content or the way the yarn was spun. Also, yarns with natural fibers weigh less or more depending on the amount of moisture in the environment, since those fibers readily absorb whatever ambient moisture is in the air.

But weight can be a good point of comparison if you're checking out two different yarns in the same class and want a better idea of how they differ. Simply compare the actual weight and yardage of each skein. You may be surprised. I found two bulky yarns that looked relatively similar and both came in fifty-gram skeins. The first, made of pure wool, had eighty yards per skein; the second, a blend of wool and lighter fibers, had 120 yards—or 50 percent more yarn. Knit the same garment out of each yarn and the first will weigh 50 percent more because you're using twice as much yarn.

The more you use this language, the more familiar it will become. In the meantime, make a cheat sheet of all the weights, gauges, and needle sizes. When you're at a crowded LYS, fall in love with a shawl pattern, and are told that it uses fingering-weight yarn, you can quickly glance at your notes and find—with total confidence—all the info for your ideal yarn.

CLARA PARKES explores new and unusual yarns each week in her online magazine, *Knitter's Review*, and in her books, *The Knitter's Book of Yarn: The Ultimate Guide to Choosing, Using, and Enjoying Yarn* (Potter Craft, 2007), *The Knitter's Book of Wool: The Ultimate Guide to Understanding, Using, and Loving this Most Fabulous Fiber* (Potter Craft, 2009), and *The Knitter's Book of Socks: The Yarn Lover's Ultimate Guide to Creating Socks that Fit Well, Feel Great, and Last a Lifetime* (Potter Craft, 2011).

ONLINE RESOURCE The Craft Yarn Council of America also offers valuable information about yarn types; find this and more online at yarnstandards.com.

Ah, the CPH—a box hood and simple rope cable climbing on a rustic tweed! This design ranks as the most popular single pattern produced by Interweave. Designer Heather Lodinsky hinted once that royalties from online sales of the pattern had paid for her daughter's college tuition. We've reworked the original here in fuchsia and incorporated expanded sizing. *designed by* **HEATHER LODINSKY**

central park hoodie

FINISHED SIZE
About 32 (36, 40, 44, 48, 52, 56, 60)" (81.5 [91.5 [101.5, 112, 122, 132, 142, 152.5] cm) bust circumference. Hoodie shown measures 36" (91.5 cm).

YARN
Worsted weight (#4 Medium).

SHOWN HERE Tahki Yarns Donegal Tweed (100% wool; 183 yd [167 m]/110 g): #810 fuchsia, 6 (7, 8, 9, 10, 16, 18, 20) skeins (see Notes).

NEEDLES
BODY, SLEEVES + HOOD size U.S. 8 (5 mm). **EDGING** size U.S. 6 (4 mm). **FRONT BANDS AND HOOD EDGING** size U.S. 6 (4 mm): 32" to 40" (80 to 100 cm) circular (cir).

Adjust needle size if necessary to obtain the correct gauge.

NOTIONS
Cable needle (cn); markers (m); stitch holders; tapestry needle; 5 to 7 buttons (optional); size G/6 (4.25 mm) crochet hook (optional).

GAUGE
17 sts and 24 rows = 4" (10 cm) in St st on larger needles (see Notes if making one of the three largest sizes).

NOTES
● The original pattern only went up to size 48" (122 cm), then three more sizes were added later; hence some of the differences between the smaller sizes and the three largest.

● For the three largest sizes, the pattern was configured with a stitch gauge of 18 stitches per 4" (10 cm). If you are making one of these sizes, adjust needle size as necessary to achieve this gauge.

● For the three largest sizes, the instructions differ in some places. It may be helpful to go through the pattern and highlight your relevant directions before beginning.

BACK

With smaller needles, CO 78 (86, 94, 102, 110, 122, 138, 146) sts. Cont for your size as foll:

SIZES 32 (36, 40, 44, 48)"
(81.5 [91.5, 101.5, 112, 122] CM) ONLY

Row 1 (RS) *K2, p2; rep from * to last 2 sts, k2.

Row 2 (WS) *P2, k2; rep from * to last 2 sts, p2.

SIZES 52 (56, 60)"
(132 [142, 152.5] CM) ONLY

Row 1 (RS) *P2, k2; rep from * to last 2 sts, p2.

Row 2 (WS) *K2, p2; rep from * to last 2 sts, k2.

ALL SIZES

Rep Rows 1 and 2 until piece measures 4 (4, 4, 4, 4, 4¼, 4½, 4½)" (10 [10, 10, 10, 10, 11, 11.5, 11.5] cm) from CO, ending with a WS row. Change to larger needles.

Row 1 (RS) K14 (14, 14, 18, 18, 24, 32, 36), place marker (pm), work Row 1 of Chart A (page 24) over 10 sts, pm, k6 (10, 14, 14, 18, 18, 18, 18), pm, work Row 1 of Chart B over 18 sts, pm, k6 (10, 14, 14, 18, 18, 18, 18), pm, work Row 1 of Chart C over 10 sts, pm, k14 (14, 14, 18, 18, 24, 32, 36).

Row 2 (WS) P14 (14, 14, 18, 18, 24, 32, 36), work Row 2 of Chart C to next m, p6 (10, 14, 14, 18, 18, 18, 18), work Row 2 of Chart B to next m, p6 (10, 14, 14, 18, 18, 18, 18), work Row 2 of Chart A to next m, p14 (14, 14, 18, 18, 24, 32, 36).

Cont in patt as established until piece measures 13½ (14, 14, 14½, 14½, 16¼, 17,

17¾)" (34.5 [35.5, 35.5, 37, 37, 41.5, 43, 45] cm) from CO, ending with a WS row.

Shape Armholes

BO 4 (5, 6, 7, 8, 8, 8, 8) sts at beg of next 2 rows, then BO 2 sts at beg of foll 2 rows—66 (72, 78, 84, 90, 102, 118, 126) sts rem.

Dec row (RS) K2, ssk, work in patt to last 4 sts, k2tog, k2—2 sts dec'd.

Work 1 WS row. Rep the last 2 rows 1 (1, 1, 1, 1, 3, 5, 7) more time(s), then work Dec row every other RS row (i.e., every 4th row) 0 (0, 0, 0, 0, 7, 7, 7) times—62 (68, 74, 80, 86, 80, 92, 96) sts rem. Work even in patt until armholes measure 8 (8, 8½, 8½, 9, 8½, 9¼, 9¾)" (20.5 [20.5, 21.5, 21.5, 23, 21.5, 23.5, 25] cm), ending with a WS row.

Shape Shoulders

Keeping in patt, BO 5 (6, 6, 7, 8, 6, 7, 8) sts at beg of next 6 rows, then BO 0 (0, 0, 0, 0, 5, 8, 7) sts at beg of foll 2 rows—32 (32, 38, 38, 38, 34, 34, 34) sts rem.

Place all sts on a holder for back neck.

LEFT FRONT

With smaller needles, CO 36 (40, 44, 48, 52, 55, 63, 71) sts. Cont for your size as foll.

SIZES 32 (36, 40, 44, 48)" (81.5 [91.5, 101.5, 112, 122] CM) ONLY

Row 1 (RS) *K2, p2; rep from * to end of row.

Row 2 (WS) *K2, p2; rep from * to end.

SIZES 52 (56, 60)" (132 [142, 152.5] CM) ONLY

Row 1 (RS) *P2, k2; rep from* to last 3 sts, p2, k1.

Row 2 (WS) P1, k2, *p2, k2; rep from * to end.

ALL SIZES

Rep Rows 1 and 2 until piece measures 4 (4, 4, 4, 4, 4¼, 4½, 4½)" (10 [10, 10, 10, 10, 11, 11.5, 11.5] cm) from CO, ending with a WS row. Change to larger needles.

Row 1 (RS) K14 (14, 14, 18, 18, 24, 32, 36), pm, work Row 1 of Chart A over 10 sts, pm, k2 (6, 10, 10, 14, 10, 10, 14), pm, work Row 1 of Chart A over 10 sts, k0 (0, 0, 0, 0, 1, 1, 1).

Row 2 (WS) P0 (0, 0, 0, 0, 1, 1, 1), work Row 2 of Chart A to next m, p2 (6, 10, 10, 14, 10, 10, 14), work Row 2 of Chart A to next m, p14 (14, 14, 18, 18, 24, 32, 36).

Cont in patt as established until piece measures 13½ (14, 14, 14½, 14½, 16¼, 17, 17¾)" (34.5 [35.5, 35.5, 37, 37, 41.5, 43, 45] cm) from CO, ending with a WS row.

Shape Armhole + Neck

Note Depending on the size you're working, several things happen at the same time; read all the way through the foll section before proceeding.

Next row (RS) BO 4 (5, 6, 7, 8, 8, 8, 8) sts, work in patt to end.

Work 1 WS row even in patt.

Next row (RS) BO 2 sts, work in patt to end.

Work 1 WS row.

Dec row (RS) K2, ssk, work in patt to end—1 st dec'd.

Work 1 WS row. Rep last 2 rows 1 (1, 1, 1, 1, 3, 5, 7) more time(s), then rep Dec row

right front & back

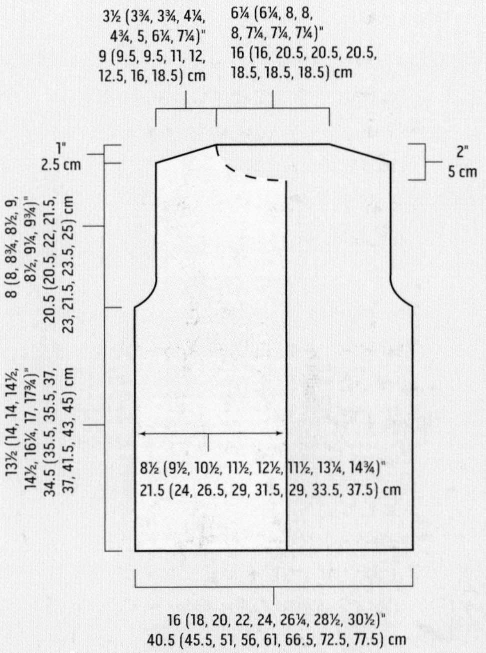
3½ (3¾, 3¾, 4¼, 4¾, 5, 6¼, 7¼)"
9 (9.5, 9.5, 11, 12, 12.5, 16, 18.5) cm
6¼ (6¼, 8, 8, 8, 7¼, 7¼, 7¼)"
16 (16, 20.5, 20.5, 20.5, 18.5, 18.5, 18.5) cm
1"
2.5 cm
2"
5 cm
8 (8, 8¾, 8½, 9, 8½, 9¼, 9¾)"
20.5 (20.5, 22, 21.5, 23, 21.5, 23.5, 25) cm
13½ (14, 14, 14½, 14½, 16¼, 17, 17¾)"
34.5 (35.5, 35.5, 37, 37, 41.5, 43, 45) cm
8½ (9½, 10½, 11½, 12½, 11½, 13¼, 14¾)"
21.5 (24, 26.5, 29, 31.5, 29, 33.5, 37.5) cm
16 (18, 20, 22, 24, 26¼, 28¼, 30½)"
40.5 (45.5, 51, 56, 61, 66.5, 72.5, 77.5) cm

sleeve

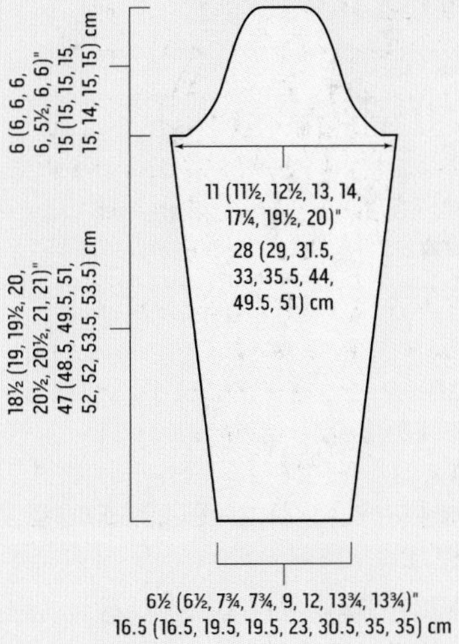
6 (6, 6, 6, 6, 5½, 6, 6)"
15 (15, 15, 15, 15, 14, 15, 15) cm
11 (11½, 12½, 13, 14, 17¼, 19½, 20)"
28 (29, 31.5, 33, 35.5, 44, 49.5, 51) cm
18½ (19, 19½, 20, 20½, 20½, 21, 21)"
47 (48.5, 49.5, 51, 52, 52, 53.5, 53.5) cm
6½ (6½, 7¾, 7¾, 9, 12, 13¾, 13¾)"
16.5 (16.5, 19.5, 19.5, 23, 30.5, 35, 35) cm

every other RS row (i.e., every 4th row) 0 (0, 0, 0, 0, 7, 7, 7) times—28 (31, 34, 37, 40, 34, 40, 46) sts rem. *At the same time* work for your size as foll.

SIZES 32 (36, 40, 44, 48)"
(81.5 [91.5, 101.5, 112, 122] CM) ONLY
Work even in patt until armhole measures 6 (6, 6½, 6½, 7)" (15 [15, 16.5, 16.5, 18] cm), ending with a RS row.

Next row (WS) Work in patt across 10 sts, then place these sts on a holder.

Make note of last cable row worked in charts. Work to end of row. Keeping in patt, BO 1 (1, 2, 2, 2) st(s) at neck edge every other row 3 times—15 (18, 18, 21, 24) sts rem. Work even in patt until front measures same as back to beg of shoulder shaping, ending with a WS row. Skip to Shape Shoulder.

SIZES 52 (56, 60)"
(132, 142, 152.5] CM) ONLY
Work as established until armhole measures 5 (6, 6½)" (12.5 [15, 16.5] cm), ending with a WS row.

Next row (RS) Work in patt to last 11 sts, including any armhole shaping, then place last 11 sts of row on holder.

Cont working rem sts in patt—23 (29, 35) sts rem after armhole shaping is completed. Work even in patt until armhole measures 8½ (9¼, 9¾)" (21.5 [23.5, 25] cm), ending with a WS row.

Shape Shoulder

Keeping in patt, BO 5 (6, 6, 7, 8, 6, 7, 8) sts at beg of next 3 RS rows, then BO 0 (0, 0, 0, 0, 5, 8, 11) sts at beg of next RS row—no sts rem.

CHART A

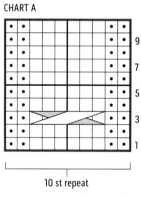

10 st repeat

CHART B

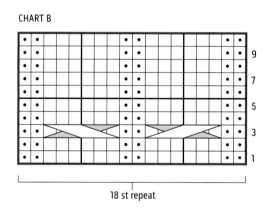

18 st repeat

CHART C

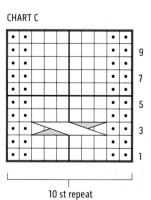

10 st repeat

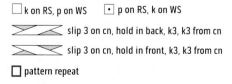

□ k on RS, p on WS   · p on RS, k on WS

⟋⟍ slip 3 on cn, hold in back, k3, k3 from cn

⟍⟋ slip 3 on cn, hold in front, k3, k3 from cn

□ pattern repeat

RIGHT FRONT

With smaller needles, CO 36 (40, 44, 48, 52, 55, 63, 71) sts. Cont for your size as foll.

SIZES 32 (36, 40, 44, 48)"
(81.5 [91.5, 101.5, 112, 122] CM) ONLY

Row 1 (RS) *P2, k2; rep from * to end of row.

Row 2 (WS) *P2, k2; rep from * to end of row.

SIZES 52 (56, 60)"
(132, 142, 152.5] CM) ONLY

Row 1 (RS) K1, p2, *k2, p2; rep from * to end.

Row 2 (WS) *K2, p2; rep from * to last 3 sts, k2, p1.

ALL SIZES

Rep Rows 1 and 2 until piece measures (4, 4, 4, 4, 4¼, 4½, 4½)" (10 [10, 10, 10, 10, 11, 11.5, 11.5] cm) from CO, ending with a WS row. Change to larger needles.

Row 1 (RS) K0 (0, 0, 0, 0, 1, 1, 1), work Row 1 of Chart C over 10 sts, pm, k2 (6, 10, 10, 14, 10, 10, 14), pm, work Row 1 of Chart C over 10 sts, pm, k14 (14, 14, 18, 18, 24, 32, 36).

Row 2 (WS) P14 (14, 14, 18, 18, 24, 32, 36), work Row 2 of Chart C to m, p2 (6, 10, 10, 14, 10, 10, 14), work Row 2 of Chart C to m, p0 (0, 0, 0, 0, 1, 1, 1).

Cont in patt as established until piece measures 13½ (14, 14, 14½, 14½, 16¼, 17, 17¾)" (34.5 [35.5, 35.5, 37, 37, 41.5, 43, 45] cm) from CO, ending with a RS row.

Shape Armhole

Note Depending on the size you're working, several things happen at the same time; read all the way through the foll section before proceeding.

Next row (WS) BO 4 (5, 6, 7, 8, 8, 8, 8) sts, work in patt to end.

Work 1 RS row even in patt.

Next row (WS) BO 2 sts, work in patt to end.

Next row (RS) Work in patt to last 4 sts, k2tog, k2—1 st dec'd.

Work 1 WS row. Rep the last 2 rows 1 (1, 1, 1, 1, 3, 5, 7) more time(s), then rep Dec row every other RS row (i.e., every 4th row) 0 (0, 0, 0, 0, 7, 7, 7) times—28 (31, 34, 37, 40, 34, 40, 46) sts rem. *At the same time* work for your size as foll.

SIZES 32 (36, 40, 44, 48)"
(81.5 [91.5, 101.5, 112, 122] CM) ONLY

Work even in patt until armhole measures 6 (6, 6½, 6½, 7)" (15 [15, 16.5, 16.5, 18] cm), ending with a WS row.

Next row (RS) Work in patt across 10 sts, then place these sts on a holder.

Make note of last cable row worked in charts (should match left front). Work to end of row. Keeping in patt, BO 1 (1, 2, 2, 2) st(s) at neck edge every other row 3 times—15 (18, 18, 21, 24) sts rem. Work even in patt until front measures same as back to beg of shoulder shaping, ending with a RS row. Skip to Shape Shoulder.

SIZES 52 (56, 60)"
(132 [142, 152.5] CM) ONLY

Work as established until armhole measures 5 (6, 6½)" (12.5 [15, 16.5] cm), ending with a RS row.

Next row (WS) Work in patt to last 11 sts, then place last 11 sts of row on holder.

Cont working rem sts in patt—23 (29, 35) sts rem after armhole shaping is completed.

Work even in patt until armhole measures 8½ (9¼, 9¾)" (21.5 [23.5, 25] cm), ending with a WS row.

Shape Shoulder

Keeping in patt, BO 5 (6, 6, 7, 8, 6, 7, 8) sts at beg of next 3 WS rows, then BO 0 (0, 0, 0, 0, 5, 8, 11) sts at beg of next WS row—no sts rem.

SLEEVES

With smaller needles, CO 38 (38, 46, 46, 54, 54, 62, 62) sts. Work ribbing for all sizes as foll:

Row 1 (RS) *K2, p2; rep from * to last 2 sts, k2.

Row 2 (WS) *P2, k2; rep from * to last 2 sts, p2.

Cont in rib as established until piece measures 5 (5, 5, 5, 5, 4¼, 4¼, 4¼)" (12.5 [12.5, 12.5, 12.5, 12.5, 11, 11, 11] cm) from CO, ending with a WS row. Change to larger needles.

Row 1 (RS) K10 (10, 14, 14, 18, 18, 22, 22), pm, work Row 1 of Chart B over 18 sts, pm, k10 (10, 14, 14, 18, 18, 22, 22).

Row 2 (WS) P10 (10, 14, 14, 18, 18, 22, 22), work Row 2 of Chart B to next m, p10 (10, 14, 14, 18, 18, 22, 22).

Cont in patt and *at the same time* inc 1 st each end of needle every 8th row 9 (10, 9, 10, 9, 8, 8, 7) times, then every 4th row 0 (0, 0, 0, 0, 4, 5, 7) times—56 (58, 64, 66, 72, 78, 88, 90) sts. Work even in patt until sleeve measures 18½ (19, 19½, 20, 20½, 20½, 21, 21)" (47 [48.5, 49.5, 51, 52, 52, 53.5, 53.5] cm) from CO, ending with a WS row.

Shape Cap

Cont in patt, BO 4 (5, 6, 7, 8, 8, 8, 8) sts at beg of next 2 rows, then BO 2 sts at beg of foll 2 rows, then BO 2 sts at beg of foll 0 (0, 0, 0, 0, 2, 2) rows—44 (44, 48, 48, 52, 58, 64, 66) sts rem. Cont for your size as foll.

SIZES 32 (36, 40, 44, 48)" (81.5 [91.5, 101.5, 112, 122] CM) ONLY

Dec row (RS) K2, ssk, work to last 4 sts, k2tog, k2—2 sts dec'd.

Rep Dec row every RS row 3 times, then every 4th row (i.e., every 2nd RS row) 5 times—26 (26, 30, 30, 34) sts rem. BO 2 sts at beg of next 4 rows—18 (18, 22, 22, 26) sts rem. BO all sts.

SIZES 52 (56, 60)" (132, 142, 152.5] CM) ONLY

Dec row (RS) K2, ssk, work to last 4 sts, k2tog, k2—2 sts dec'd.

Rep Dec row on every RS row 11 (12, 12) more times—34 (38, 40) sts rem. BO 2 sts at beg of next 4 rows—26 (30, 32) sts rem. BO all sts.

FINISHING

Block pieces to measurements. With yarn threaded on a tapestry needle, sew shoulder seams.

Hood

With larger needles, RS facing, and starting at right front neck, work across 10 (10, 10, 10, 10, 11, 11, 11) held sts in patt, pick up and knit 11 (11, 14, 14, 14, 17, 21, 23) sts along right-front neckline (for three largest sizes, this is the straight edge along the right front), k32 (32, 38, 38, 38, 34, 34, 34) held back sts, pick up and knit 11 (11, 14, 14, 14, 17, 21, 23) sts along left-front neck, then work rem 10 (10, 10, 10, 10, 11,

11, 11) held sts in patt—74 (74, 86, 86, 86, 90, 98, 102) sts total.

Next row (WS) Work charted sts in patt, pm, purl to next cabled section, pm, work in patt to end.

Note You can cont the cable onto the hood (as shown in photo) or cease working cable patt and work hood in plain St st.

Cont in patt until hood measures 11 (11, 11½, 11½, 12, 12¼, 12¼ 12½)" (28 [28, 29, 29, 30.5, 31, 31, 31.5] cm) from shoulder, ending with a RS row.

Next row (WS) Work 37 (37, 43, 43, 43, 45, 49, 51) sts, pm, work rem 37 (37, 43, 43, 43, 45, 49, 51) sts.

Dec row (RS) Work to 3 sts before m, k2tog, k1, sl m, k1, ssk, work to end —2 sts dec'd.

Rep Dec row every RS row 4 more times—64 (64, 76, 76, 76, 80, 88, 92) sts rem. Use the three-needle method (see Glossary) to BO sts tog.

Front Bands + Hood Edging

Work for your size as foll.

SIZES 32 (36, 40, 44, 48)" (81.5 [91.5, 101.5, 112, 122] CM) ONLY:

With smaller cir needle, RS facing, and starting at upper edge of hood, pick up and knit 146 (150, 154, 158, 162) sts evenly spaced to the lower bottom edge of the left front.

Next row (WS) *P2, k2; rep from * to last 2 sts, p2.

Work in rib as established until band measures 1½" (3.8 cm). BO all sts in rib. With smaller needles, RS facing, and starting at lower edge of right front, pick up and knit 146 (150, 154, 158, 162) sts

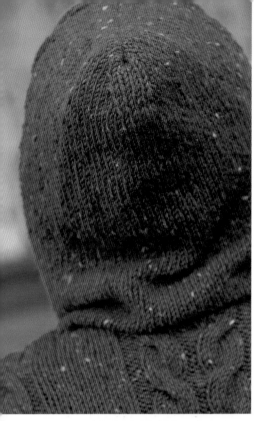

evenly spaced along edge of right front and edge of right side of hood.

Next row (WS) *P2, k2; rep from * to last 2 sts, p2.

Work in rib as established until band measures 1½" (3.8 cm). BO all sts in rib.

OPTIONAL BUTTON/BUTTONHOLE

After working the left-front band, mark the placement for 5 or 6 buttons along band. On right-front band, work rib for 3 rows. On the 4th row, BO 2 sts at points marked for buttonhole placement. On next row, CO 2 sts above each place where sts were BO. Cont in rib until band measures 1½" (3.8 cm). BO all sts in rib.

Sew top of hood tog. Sew buttons opposite buttonholes. Skip to All Sizes.

SIZES 52 (56, 60)" (132 [142, 152.5] CM) ONLY

With smaller cir needle, RS facing, and beg at bottom corner of right front, pick up and knit 181 (189, 197) sts evenly spaced along right front and right-front edge of hood, ending at seam at top of hood. Pick up and knit 181 (189, 197) sts evenly spaced down left-front edge of hood and left front—362 (378, 394) sts total.

Next row (WS) *P2, k2; rep from * to last 2 sts, p2.

Cont in rib until band measures 2½" (6.5 cm). BO all sts in rib.

OPTIONAL CROCHET BUTTON LOOPS

With size G/6 (4 mm) crochet hook, join yarn with sl st (see Glossary for crochet instructions) to right front band edge, about ½" (1.3 cm) up from the bottom edge.

Ch 7, join with sl st to band edge about 1" (2.5 cm) above starting point, turn, sc in each ch, join with sl st to knitted edge, fasten off. Keeping loops spaced about 1" (2.5 cm) apart, rep button loops along right-front edge, ending at a point level with the underarm—you should be able to fit 6–7 button loops. Sew buttons to corresponding points on left front band, closer to the body of the left front.

ALL SIZES

Sew sleeve caps into armholes. Sew side seams and sleeve seams. Weave in loose ends.

HEATHER LODINSKY

lives in Buffalo, New York, with her husband, two daughters, and an extremely well-trained feline assistant. She has been a professional knitwear and crochet designer for fifteen years and designs for major yarn companies. Heather has also taught walk-in knitting classes three times a week at her local yarn shop for fifteen years. She is author of *150 Knit and Crochet Motifs* (Interweave, 2011).

Originally published in Fall 2006, then updated for KnittingDaily.com in 2008

cables

KEN FRANTZ

PUT A NEW TWIST ON your stitches, literally! Cables are deceptively simple. They're formed by reversing the order in which you knit the stitches on your needles. You're leapfrogging one set of stitches to knit the following ones, and then returning to the ones you skipped. The result is a visually twisted set of stitches.

DO THE TWIST

Cables can twist to the right or the left. Their direction depends on whether you hold the cable needle in front of your work or at the back of your work.

To twist your cable to the right, put the cable needle behind your work and knit in front of it. To twist your cable to the left, put the needle in front of your work and knit behind it.

When you're first starting out, you'll want to turn your cables with a cable needle. This is a short needle (normally about 3" [7.5 cm] long) with edges that are either thicker than the center of the needle or bent at a slight angle to keep your stitches from sliding off. You can use a finer needle than your working needles but not a thicker one.

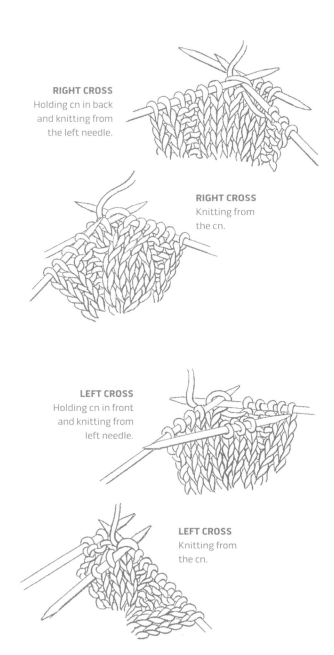

RIGHT CROSS
Holding cn in back and knitting from the left needle.

RIGHT CROSS
Knitting from the cn.

LEFT CROSS
Holding cn in front and knitting from left needle.

LEFT CROSS
Knitting from the cn.

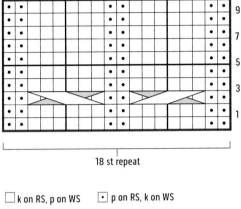

18 st repeat

☐ k on RS, p on WS   ⊡ p on RS, k on WS

▷◁ slip 3 on cn, hold in back, k3, k3 from cn

▷◁ slip 3 on cn, hold in front, k3, k3 from cn

☐ pattern repeat

Cables are normally knitted in stockinette stitch bordered by purl stitches that highlight the smooth sculptural quality of the cable. Because cables cause the surrounding fabric to pull inward, patterns will have extra width to account for this.

CHARTS 101

Cable patterns are often written in chart form to save space. If you see a chart, don't panic—they're actually quite easy to decipher once you get the hang of them.

Charts tell how many stitches are in your cable and which way to twist them. The "X" shape spans all the stitches in the cable. The angle of the top leg of the X tells you where to hold your cable needle—in front or back of your work and, therefore, which way the cable will slant. To twist your cable to the right, put the cable needle behind your work and knit in front of it.

When the top leg angles to the right, you will have a right-slanting cable; when the top leg angles to the left, you will have a left-slanting cable. The key to a chart will tell you how to work the actual cable.

TRY IT

Let's do a practice swatch using the back center cable from Heather Lodinsky's hooded pullover (page 20). Gather some yarn (worsted weight is ideal), needles, and a cable needle. Cast on 18 stitches, then begin following the chart at left.

1. **Rows 1 and 2:** These are simple rows with knit and purl stitches that will define the area where your cable will be turned in later rows.

2. **Row 3:** (cable turn row) P2. The first cable is a right-slanting cable, so slip 3 stitches onto a cable needle and move it behind your work. Knit the next 3 stitches on your left needle, then knit the 3 stitches from your cable needle. You can either knit them straight off the cable needle or slip the stitches onto your left needle and then knit them. P2.

Now it's time for the second cable, which is a left-slanting cable. Slip 3 stitches onto a cable needle, but this time you'll want to hold the cable needle in front of your work. Knit the next 3 stitches on your left needle, then knit the 3 stitches from your cable needle. P2 and you're done! You've turned your first cables.

3. Follow the remaining 7 rows on the chart to finish one full cable repeat. These plain rows are needed to give clear definition to your cable. A general rule of thumb is that you turn a cable every X rows, where X is the total number of stitches in the cable. But as you see from our swatch, you can also have more plain rows between cable turns.

MORE ABOUT CABLING
Inspired Cable Knits, Fiona Ellis (Potter Craft); *Cable Knitting Handbook,* Annie Maloney (The Knitter's Craft Series); *Power Cables,* Lily M. Chin (Interweave).

The Geodesic was an overnight sensation. One of three designs for Connie Chang Chinchio's *Knitscene* collection, this light-as-air jacket, with its military-inspired bodice tucks, was worked up in the yarn du jour at the time—Malabrigo Lace. It does require some advanced skills, but it's so appealing that knitters of every stripe have taken a go at it, with fine results.

designed by **CONNIE CHANG CHINCHIO**

geodesic cardigan

FINISHED SIZE
About 31½ (34½, 38, 42, 46, 50, 54)" (80 [87.5, 96.5, 106.5, 117, 127, 137] cm) bust circumference, with about 3" (7.5 cm) gap at center front. Sweater shown measures 34½" (87.5 cm).

YARN
Lace weight (#0 Lace).

SHOWN HERE Malabrigo Lace (100% merino; 470 yd [430 m]/50 g): #56 olive, 2 (2, 3, 3, 3, 3, 4) skeins.

NEEDLES
Size U.S. 6 (4 mm): 24" (60 cm) circular (cir) and set of 4 or 5 double-pointed (dpn).

Adjust needle size if necessary to obtain the correct gauge.

NOTIONS
Markers (m; in one color to mark seams and a different color to mark darts); stitch holders; waste yarn for provisional cast-on; tapestry needle.

GAUGE
24 sts and 40 rows = 4" (10 cm) in St st.

NOTES
- The body is worked in one piece to the underarms with a faux slip-stitch "seam" at each side.

- Tucks are made by working rows of stockinette stitch flanked by two reverse-stockinette rows. The tucks begin with a reverse-stockinette row, then seven rows of stockinette, then one reverse-stockinette row, then the live stitches are worked together with the bumps on the wrong side above the first reverse-stockinette row. Two sets of short-rows are made in each tuck so as not to create extra fabric in the body stitches adjacent to the tucks. See Stitch Guide for more details.

- The two center front edge stitches of the left and right fronts are worked in garter stitch throughout, including the tucks.

stitch guide

LEFT-FRONT TUCK (worked over 18 [21, 22, 24, 24, 26, 26] sts)

Work in short-rows (see Glossary) as foll:

Row 1 (WS; short-row) K18 (21, 22, 24, 24, 26, 26), wrap next st, turn.

Row 2 (RS) K18 (21, 22, 24, 24, 26, 26).

Row 3 (WS) K2, p16 (19, 20, 22, 22, 24, 24), work wrap tog with wrapped st, then work body in patt.

Row 4 (RS) K18 (21, 22, 24, 24, 26, 26).

Row 5 (WS; short-row) K2, p16 (19, 20, 22, 22, 24, 24), wrap next st, turn.

Row 6 (RS) K18 (21, 22, 24, 24, 26, 26).

Row 7 (WS) K2, p16 (19, 20, 22, 22, 24, 24), work wrap tog with wrapped st, then work body in patt.

Row 8 (RS) K18 (21, 22, 24, 24, 26, 26).

Row 9 (WS) K18 (21, 22, 24, 24, 26, 26), then work body in patt.

Row 10 (RS) Fold tuck with WS tog. *With left needle tip, pick up purl bump on WS of tuck above Row 1 of tuck, k2tog (purl bump with first st on needle); rep from * 17 (20, 21, 23, 23, 25, 25) more times, then work body in patt.

Rows 11–18 Work even in St st.
Rep Rows 1–18 for pattern.

RGHT-FRONT TUCK (18 [21, 22, 24, 24, 26, 26] sts)

Work in short-rows as foll:

Row 1 (WS) K18 (21, 22, 24, 24, 26, 26).

Row 2 (RS; short-row) K18 (21, 22, 24, 24, 26, 26), wrap next st, turn.

Row 3 (WS) Purl to last 2 sts, k2.

Row 4 (RS) K18 (21, 22, 24, 24, 26, 26), work wrap tog with wrapped st (then work body in patt).

Row 5 (WS) Purl to last 2 sts, k2.

Row 6 (RS; short-row) K18 (21, 22, 24, 24, 26, 26), wrap next st, turn.

Row 7 (WS) Purl to last 2 sts, k2.

Row 8 (RS) K18 (21, 22, 24, 24, 26, 26), work wrap tog with wrapped st (then work body in patt).

Row 9 (WS) K18 (21, 22, 24, 24, 26, 26).

Row 10 (RS) Fold tuck with WS tog. *With left needle, pick up purl bump on WS of tuck above Row 1 of tuck, k2tog (purl bump with first st on needle); rep from * 17 (20, 21, 23, 23, 25, 25) more times (then work body in patt).

Rows 11–18 Work in St st.
Rep Rows 1–18 for pattern.

BODY

With cir needle, CO 190 (210, 230, 254, 278, 302, 326) sts. Do not join.

Set-up row (RS) K28 (31, 34, 37, 41, 45, 48), place marker (pm) for dart, k19 (21, 23, 26, 28, 30, 33), pm for seam, sl 1, pm for seam, k19 (21, 23, 26, 28, 30, 33), pm for dart, k56 (62, 68, 74, 82, 90, 96), pm for dart, k19 (21, 23, 26, 28, 30, 33), pm for seam, sl 1, pm for seam, k19 (21, 23, 26, 28, 30, 33), pm for dart, knit to end.

Next row (WS) Knit to seam m, sl m, p1, sl m, knit to next seam m, sl m, p1, sl m, knit to end.

Next row (RS) Knit to seam m, sl m, sl 1, sl m, knit to next seam m, sl m, sl 1, sl m, knit to end.

Next row (WS) K2, purl to last 2 sts, k2.

Rep the last 2 rows until piece measures 3" (7.5 cm) from CO, ending with a WS row.

Shape Waist

Note Tucks beg before waist shaping ends and neck shaping begs before tucks are completed; read the foll sections all the way through before proceeding.

Dec row (RS) Cont working seam sts as established, knit to 2 sts before dart m, k2tog, sl m, work to next dart m, sl m, ssk, work to 2 sts before next dart m, k2tog, sl m, work to next dart m, sl m, ssk, knit to end—4 sts dec'd.

Rep dec row every 8th row 4 (2, 2, 2, 4, 4, 4) more times, then every 10th row 0 (2, 2, 2, 0, 0, 0) times—170 (190, 210, 234, 258, 282, 306) sts rem. Work even for 2" (5 cm), ending with a WS row—piece measures about 8¼ (8¾, 8¾, 8¾, 8¼, 8¼, 8¼)" (21 [22, 22, 22, 21, 21, 21] cm) from CO.

Inc row (RS) Work to dart m, M1 (see Glossary), sl m, work to next dart m, sl m, M1, work to next dart m, M1, sl m, work to next dart m, sl m, M1, work to end—4 sts inc'd.

Rep inc row every 12th row 4 more times—190 (210, 230, 254, 278, 302, 326) sts.

Tucks

At the same time when piece measures 10¼ (11, 10½, 10½, 10, 9½, 9½)" (26 [28, 26.5, 26.5, 25.5, 24, 24] cm) from CO, ending with a RS row, beg tucks as foll:

(WS) Work Rows 1–3 of left-front tuck (see Stitch Guide), work to last 18 (21, 22, 24, 24, 26, 26) sts, work Row 1 of right-front tuck (see Stitch Guide). Cont working tucks over first and last 18 (21, 22, 24, 24, 26, 26) sts in this manner until there are 7 (8, 8, 9, 9, 10, 10) tucks on each front, then work these sts in St st with garter st edging.

Shape Neck

Note Neck shaping begs before, during, or after the beg of armhole shaping, depending on size; read the foll section all the way through before proceeding.

Also at the same time when piece measures 13¼ (14¼, 14½, 14¾, 14¾, 15, 15)" (33.5 [36, 37, 37.5, 37.5, 38, 38] cm) from CO, ending with a WS row, shape neck as foll:

Dec row (RS) Work 18 (21, 22, 24, 24, 26, 26) sts in patt, ssk, work to last 20 (23, 24, 26, 26, 28, 28) sts of left front, k2tog, work to end—2 sts dec'd for neck.

Rep dec row every 4th row (don't count the short-rows in the tucks as rows) 17 (18, 18, 19, 19, 20, 20) more times—18 (19, 19, 20, 20, 21, 21) sts dec'd each neck edge.

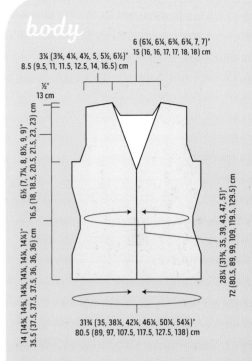

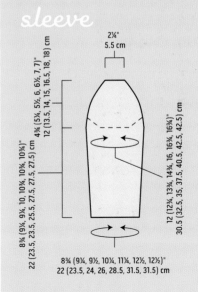

geodesic cardigan **33**

Also at the same time when piece measures 14 (14¾, 14¾, 14¾, 14¼, 14¼, 14¼)" (35.5 [37.5, 37.5, 37.5, 36, 36, 36] cm) from CO, ending with a WS row, divide for armholes as foll: (RS) Work to seam m, k2tog (seam st with first st of back; remove seam m), BO 5 (5, 6, 8, 9, 9, 9) sts, knit to 1 st before next seam m, k2tog (last st of back with seam st; remove seam m), turn.

BACK

Work back sts back and forth in rows as foll:

With WS facing, BO 5 (5, 6, 8, 9, 9, 9) sts—84 (94, 102, 110, 120, 132, 144) sts rem for back.

Armhole dec row (RS) K1, ssk, knit to last 3 sts, k2tog, k1—2 sts dec'd.

Rep armhole dec row every RS row 4 (5, 6, 7, 9, 11, 11) more times—74 (82, 88, 94, 100, 108, 120) sts rem for back. Work even until armholes measure 5½ (6, 6¼, 7, 7½, 8, 8)" (14 [15, 16, 18, 19, 20.5, 20.5] cm), ending with a WS row.

Shape Neck

(RS) K21 (24, 27, 29, 32, 35, 41), BO 32 (34, 34, 36, 36, 38, 38) sts, knit to end—21 (24, 27, 29, 32, 35, 41) sts rem each side. Working each side separately, dec 1 st at each neck edge every RS row 2 times—19 (22, 25, 27, 30, 33, 39) sts rem each side. Work even until armholes measure 6½ (7, 7¼, 8, 8½, 9, 9)" (16.5 [18, 18.5, 20.5, 21.5, 23, 23] cm), ending at neck edge.

Shape Shoulders

Working each side separately, work short-rows as foll:

Row 1 Work 15 (17, 18, 19, 21, 23, 27) sts, wrap next st, turn, work to end.

Row 2 Work 5 (7, 7, 7, 8, 9, 12) sts, wrap next st, turn, work to end.

Row 3 Work to end of row, working wraps tog with wrapped sts.

Place sts on holders.

LEFT FRONT

With RS facing, join yarn to armhole edge of left front. Cont neck shaping and tuck patt as established while shaping armhole as foll: (RS) BO 5 (5, 6, 8, 9, 9, 9) sts, work to end.

Work 1 WS row.

Armhole dec row (RS) K1, ssk, work to end—1 st dec'd.

Rep armhole dec row every RS row 4 (5, 6, 7, 9, 11, 11) more times. Work even until armhole measures 6½ (7, 7¼, 8, 8½, 9, 9)" (16.5 [18, 18.5, 20.5, 21.5, 23, 23] cm), ending with a RS row—19 (22, 25, 27, 30, 33, 39) sts rem.

Shape Shoulder

Work short-rows as foll:

Row 1 Work 15 (17, 18, 19, 21, 23, 27) sts, wrap next st, turn, work to end.

Row 2 Work 5 (7, 7, 7, 8, 9, 12) sts, wrap next st, turn, work to end.

Row 3 Work to end of row, working wraps tog with wrapped sts.

Place sts on holder.

RIGHT FRONT

With WS facing, join yarn to armhole edge of right front. Cont neck shaping and tuck patt as established while shaping armhole as foll: (WS) BO 5 (5, 6, 8, 9, 9, 9) sts, work to end.

Armhole dec row (RS) Work to last 3 sts, k2tog, k1—1 st dec'd.

Rep armhole dec row every RS row 4 (5, 6, 7, 9, 11, 11) more times. Work even until armhole measures 6½ (7, 7¼, 8, 8½, 9, 9)" (16.5 [18, 18.5, 20.5, 21.5, 23, 23] cm), ending with a WS row—19 (22, 25, 27, 30, 33, 39) sts rem.

Shape Shoulder

Work short-rows as foll:

Row 1 Work 15 (17, 18, 19, 21, 23, 27) sts, wrap next st, turn, work to end.

Row 2 Work 5 (7, 7, 7, 8, 9, 12) sts, wrap next st, turn, work to end.

Row 3 Work to end of row, working wraps tog with wrapped sts.

Place sts on holder.

Block to measurements. Use the three-needle method (see Glossary) to BO shoulders tog.

SLEEVES

Using the invisible-provisional method (see Glossary), CO 72 (76, 82, 88, 96, 100, 100) sts. Do not join. Work in St st for 3 rows, ending with a WS row.

Shape Cap

BO 5 (5, 6, 8, 9, 9, 9) sts at beg of next 2 rows—62 (66, 70, 72, 78, 82, 82) sts rem.

Dec row (RS) K1, ssk, knit to last 3 sts, k2tog, k1—2 sts dec'd.

Rep dec row every RS row 6 (7, 8, 8, 9, 11, 11) more times, then every 4th row 3 (3, 3, 4, 4, 4, 4) times, then every RS row 8 (9, 10, 10, 11, 12, 12) times, then every row 0 (0, 0, 0, 1, 1, 1) time—26 (26, 26, 26, 26, 24, 24) sts rem. Work 1 (1, 1, 1, 0,

0, 0) WS row even. BO 3 (3, 3, 3, 3, 2, 2) sts at beg of next 2 rows, then BO 3 sts at beg of foll 2 rows—14 sts rem for all sizes. BO all sts.

With yarn threaded on a tapestry needle, sew sleeve caps into armholes, easing any fullness at the top. Remove waste yarn from provisional CO and place live sts on dpn. Sew the short sleeve seam before the beg of the cap shaping.

Next rnd K2tog at the underarm tog to join for working in the rnd, pm for beg of rnd, knit to end of rnd—71 (75, 81, 87, 95, 99, 99) sts rem.

Dec rnd Ssk, knit to last 3 sts, k2tog, k1—2 sts dec'd.

Rep dec rnd every 6th rnd 0 (0, 7, 8, 9, 0, 0) more times, then every 8th rnd 8 (9, 4, 4, 4, 11, 11) times—53 (55, 57, 61, 67, 75, 75) sts rem. Work even until piece measures 8¾ (9¼, 9¼, 10, 10¾, 10¾, 10¾)" (22 [23.5, 23.5, 25.5, 27.5, 27.5, 27.5] cm) from underarm. Work even in garter st (alternate purl 1 rnd, knit 1 rnd) for ½" (1.3 cm). BO all sts kwise.

FINISHING
Back Neck Trim

With RS facing, pick up and knit 7 sts evenly spaced from right shoulder to back neck BO, 32 (34, 34, 36, 36, 38, 38) sts along back neck, and 7 sts to left shoulder—46 (48, 48, 50, 50, 52, 52) sts total. Knit 3 rows. With RS facing, BO all sts.

Block sleeves. Weave in loose ends. If necessary, steam-block the front edges to help them lie flat.

CONNIE CHANG CHINCHIO was the featured designer in the Winter/Spring 2010 issue of *Knitscene*. She designed a collection of three sweaters, all demonstrating her trademark elements—wearability, sporty silhouettes with feminine detailing, and refined construction methods. She lives outside New York City, where she works in finance and operates her blog and pattern shop (conniechangchinchio.com). Her first book, *Knitted Textures*, will be published by Interweave in 2012.

Originally published in Winter/Spring 2010

Oh, the shawlette. Here, a debonair bit of knitting is edged with its own cord and styled with its own geometric coolness. In a luxurious worsted weight, Kate brings the ever-popular shawl into reach for newer knitters who might be intimidated by complex charts and fine yarns. The shawl is shown reworked in a new color of the delightful Fibre Company Canopy Worsted.

designed by **KATE GAGNON OSBORN**

oscilloscope shawl

FINISHED SIZE
About 53" (134.5 cm) wide and 23¼" (59 cm) deep at center point, after blocking.

YARN
Worsted weight (#4 Medium).

SHOWN HERE The Fibre Company Canopy Worsted (50% alpaca, 30% merino, 20% bamboo; 100 yd [91 m]/50 g): macaw (navy blue), 4 skeins.

NEEDLES
Size U.S. 9 (5.5 mm): 24" (60 cm) or longer circular (cir).

Adjust needle size if necessary to obtain the correct gauge.

NOTIONS
Tapestry needle; pins for blocking.

GAUGE
14 sts and 22 rows = 4" (10 cm) in garter st, after blocking.

SHAWL

CO 6 sts. Work Rows 1–28 of Set-Up chart—19 sts. Work Rows 1–20 of Body Increase chart 6 times, adding 1 more 10-st rep each time, then work Rows 1–12 once more—85 sts. Work Rows 1–20 of Body Decrease chart 6 times, working 1 less 10-st rep each time—25 sts rem. Work Rows 1–37 of End chart—6 sts rem. BO all sts pwise.

FINISHING

With tail from CO row, join first and last sts of row (folding ends to WS of work) to form a corner. Work in same way on BO row. Weave in loose ends. Soak in wool wash and warm water for 20 minutes. Squeeze out water and pin to measurements on a flat surface.

SETUP

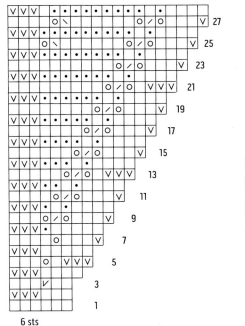

6 sts

	k on RS, p on WS
•	p on RS, k on WS
o	yo
⁄	k2tog
\	ssk
v	sl 1 wyb on RS; sl 1 wyf on WS
⌵	knit into front and back of same st
▢	pattern repeat

BODY INCREASE

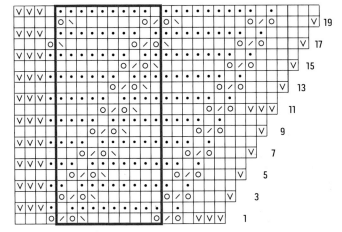

10 st repeat

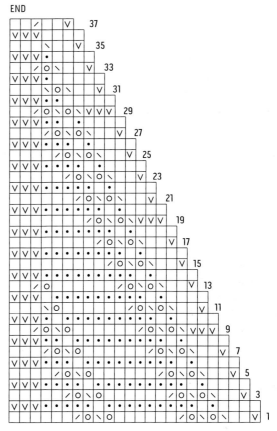

END

37
35
33
31
29
27
25
23
21
19
17
15
13
11
9
7
5
3
1

BODY DECREASE

19
17
15
13
11
9
7
5
3
1

10 st repeat

See page 40 for
more information
on designer
**KATE GAGNON
OSBORN.**

Originally
published in
Fall 2010

kate gagnon osborn

JOE COCA

KNITSCENE Choose two words to describe your aesthetic.

KATE Clean. Colorful. Modern. Traditional. (I know that's four; I'm also verbose).

While studying textile design at Philadelphia University in the mid-2000s, Kate Gagnon Osborn made the auspicious decision to pick up work at Rosie's Yarn Cellar. She began designing patterns for the downtown LYS and also met co-worker Courtney Kelley there. During this time, she started contributing designs to *Knitscene*—her first published pattern was the Tempest Beret, featured on page 42.

In 2008, Kate and Courtney started their own business, Kelbourne Woolens, as distributors of The Fibre Company's artisan yarns. They now spend their days filling yarn orders, working with dyers and mills, publishing patterns for yarn support, and more: "While we work closely together on most every aspect of the job, I focus more on the aesthetics of the brand imaging: updating the websites, planning and designing the advertising, pattern layout, graphics, and photography," says Kate.

With a new business, a new house, and being recently married, Kate took some time away from school—and quickly filled her time with co-writing a book with partner Courtney. *Vintage Modern Knits* (Interweave, 2011) celebrates the aesthetic of these two yarn-minded designers. Kate says of her work: "I love to design things that I want to wear, but I also think about the practical uses of a particular item, beginning with basic shapes and cuts, then trying to find ways to make the design unique, enjoyable to knit, and timeless." For these reasons, Kate's *Knitscene* projects have proven quite popular.

Kate went back to finish her master's degree in weaving in 2010 and is now busy as ever fixing up her early 1900s brownstone, fostering shelter dogs, and continuing the daily work at Kelbourne Woolens. We look forward to her next endeavor!

KATE'S SITES:

www.kelbournewoolens.com

www.thefibreco.com

www.kateosborndesign.com

1. In the **Conifer Shawl** (*Knitscene* Winter/Spring 2010), Kate worked an intricate top-down shawl in an unexpectedly heavy yarn. *2.* The **Oscilloscope Shawl** as seen on page 36. *3.* The **Hollywood Herringbone Pullover** (*Knitscene* Fall 2009) combines colorwork, sporty elements, and a luxe yarn for the kind of modern look that has become Kate's signature. *4.* The **Setesdal Love Hat** (*Knitscene* Winter/Spring 2011) shows off Kate's contemporary color sense.

Iridescent dyes and turning cables combine with clever shaping in Kate's aptly titled Tempest Beret. If there's one thing knitters love, it's clever shaping. Here, decreases are worked within narrowing cables to create a seamlessly patterned crown. The slouchy tam has been a favorite accessory for *Knitscene* readers, and this project serves as an exquisite example of the type.

designed by **KATE GAGNON OSBORN**

tempest beret

FINISHED SIZE
About 17" (43 cm) circumference at brim and 22" (56 cm) circumference at widest point.

YARN
Worsted weight (#4 Medium).

SHOWN HERE The Fibre Company Organik (70% merino, 15% baby alpaca, 15% silk; 100 yd [92 m]/50 g): aquatic forest, 2 skeins.

NEEDLES
HAT size U.S. 10 (6 mm): 16" (40.5 cm) circular (cir) and set of 4 double-pointed (dpn).

EDGING size U.S. 8 (5 mm): 16" (40.5 cm) cir.

Adjust needle size if necessary to obtain the correct gauge.

NOTIONS
Cable needle (cn); marker (m); 10" (25.5 cm) dinner plate for blocking; tapestry needle.

GAUGE
22 stitches and 24 rows = 4" (10 cm) in cable pattern on larger needles.

stitch guide

1/1LC Sl 1 st onto cn and hold in front, k1, k1 from cn.

1/1RC Sl 1 st onto cn and hold in back, k1, k1 from cn.

LCinc Sl 1 st onto cn and hold in front, k1f&b (see Glossary), yo, k1 from cn—2 sts inc'd.

2/2LC Sl 2 sts onto cn and hold in front, k2, k2 from cn.

2/2RC Sl 2 sts onto cn and hold in back, k2, k2 from cn.

2/2LCinc Sl 2 sts onto cn and hold in front, k1f&b (see Glossary), yo, k1, then k2 from cn.

2/2LCdec Sl 2 sts onto cn and hold in front, k2tog, k2 from cn—1 st dec'd.

2/2RCdec Sl 2 sts onto cn and hold in back, k2, k2tog from cn—1 st dec'd.

1/2LC Sl 1 st onto cn and hold in front, k2, k1 from cn.

1/2LCdec Sl 1 st onto cn and hold in front, k2tog, k1 from cn—1 st dec'd.

2/1RCdec Sl 2 sts onto cn and hold in back, k1, k2tog from cn—1 st dec'd.

BRIM PATTERN (multiple of 8 sts)

Rnds 1 and 3 *K2, p1, k4, p1; rep from *.

Rnd 2 *LC (see above), p1, k4, p1; rep from *.

Rnd 4 *LC, p1, 2/2LC (see above), p1; rep from *.

Rep Rnds 1–4 for pattern.

BODY PATTERN (multiple of 12 sts)

Rnd 1 *2/2LC, p1, 2/2RC (see above), k2, p1; rep from *.

Rnd 2 *K4, p1, k6, p1; rep from *.

Rnd 3 *K4, p1, k2, 2/2LC, p1; rep from *.

Rnd 4 Rep Rnd 2.

Rep Rnds 1–4 for pattern.

HAT

With smaller cir needle, CO 80 sts. Place marker (pm) and join for working in rnds. Work Rnds 1–4 of brim patt (see Stitch Guide) once, then work Rnds 1–3 once more.

Inc rnd *LCinc (see Stitch Guide), p1, 2/2LCinc (see Stitch Guide), p1; rep from * around—120 sts.

Change to larger cir needle.

Set-up rnd *K2, k1 through back loop (k1tbl), k1, p1, k3, k1tbl, k2, p1; rep from *.

Work Rnds 1–4 of body patt (see Stitch Guide) 5 times—piece measures about 5¼" (13.5 cm) from CO.

Shape Crown

Rnd 1 (dec rnd) *2/2LC, p1, 2/2RCdec (see Stitch Guide), k2, p1; rep from *—10 sts dec'd; 110 sts rem.

Rnd 2 *K4, p1, k5, p1; rep from *.

Rnd 3 *K4, p1, k2, 1/2LC (see Stitch Guide), p1; rep from *.

Rnd 4 Rep Rnd 2.

Rnd 5 (dec rnd) *2/2LC, p1, 2/2RCdec, k1, p1; rep from *—10 sts dec'd; 100 sts rem.

Rnd 6 *K4, p1; rep from *.

Rnd 7 *K4, p1, k2, 1/1LC, p1; rep from *.

Rnd 8 Rep Rnd 6.

Rnd 9 (dec rnd) *2/2LC, p1, 2/1RCdec (see Stitch Guide), k1, p1; rep from *—10 sts dec'd; 90 sts rem.

Rnd 10 *K4, p1, k3, p1; rep from *.

Rnd 11 *K4, p1, k1, 1/1LC, p1; rep from *.

Rnd 12 Rep Rnd 10.

Rnd 13 (dec rnd) *2/2LCdec, p1, 1/1RC, k1, p1; rep from *—10 sts dec'd; 80 sts rem.

Rnd 14 *K3, p1; rep from *.

Rnd 15 (dec rnd) *1/2LCdec, p1, k1, 1/1LC, p1; rep from *—10 sts dec'd; 70 sts rem.

Rnd 16 *K2, p1, k3, p1; rep from *.

Rnd 17 (dec rnd) *1/1LC, p1, k2tog, k1, p1; rep from *—10 sts dec'd; 60 sts rem.

Rnd 18 *K2, p1; rep from *.

Rnd 19 (dec rnd) *Ssk, p1, 1/1LC, p1; rep from *—10 sts dec'd; 50 sts rem.

Rnd 20 *K1, p1, k2, p1; rep from *.

Rnd 21 (dec rnd) *K1, p1, ssk, p1; rep from *—10 sts dec'd; 40 sts rem.

Rnd 22 *K1, p1; rep from *.

Rnd 23 (dec rnd) *Ssk, k1, p1; rep from *—10 sts dec'd; 30 sts rem.

Rnd 24 (dec rnd) *K1, ssk; rep from *—10 sts dec'd; 20 sts rem.

Rnd 25 (dec rnd) *K2tog; rep from *—10 sts rem.

Rnd 26 (dec rnd) *K2tog; rep from *—5 sts rem.

Cut yarn, leaving a 9" (23 cm) tail.

FINISHING

Thread tail on a tapestry needle, draw through rem sts, pull tight to close top, and fasten off on WS. Weave in loose ends. Stretch hat body over 10" (25.5 cm) dinner plate. Spray with warm water until wet but not dripping. Let air-dry completely before removing from plate.

See page 40 for more information on designer **KATE GAGNON OSBORN.**

Originally published in Winter 08/ Spring 09

Stockinette worked in the round, self-striping yarn, and top-down construction make for addictive knitting. This super-simple pullover is a wardrobe staple with its wide neck, shaped waist, and zenlike minimalism, thanks to unfinished edges and the organic texture of the silk-blend yarn. Noro-lovers have flocked to this design, while many other knitters have chosen to work the sweater in a solid.

designed by **DEBBIE O'NEILL**

equinox raglan

FINISHED SIZE
28¾ (32¾, 36, 40, 44, 48)" (73 [83, 91.5, 101.5, 112, 122] cm) bust circumference. Sweater shown measures 32¾" (83 cm).

YARN
Worsted weight (#4 Medium).

SHOWN HERE Noro Silk Garden (45% silk, 45% kid mohair, 10% wool; 108 yd [100 m]/ 50 g): #279 browns/blues/ deep rose, 6 (7, 8, 9, 10, 11) skeins.

NEEDLES
Sizs U.S. 7 (4.5 mm): 16" (40.5 cm), 24" (61 cm), and 32" (81.5 cm) circular (cir) and set of 4 or 5 double-pointed (dpn) each.

Adjust needle size if necessary to obtain the correct gauge.

NOTIONS
Markers (m); waste yarn for holding sts; tapestry needle.

GAUGE
20 sts and 28 rows = 4" (10 cm) in St st, worked in rnds.

YOKE

With 24" (60 cm) cir needle, CO 92 (100, 100, 104, 108, 108) sts. Place marker (pm) and join for working in rnds. Knit 1 rnd and *at the same time* pm as foll: K1 (raglan st), pm, k10 for sleeve, pm, k1 (raglan st), pm, k34 (38, 38, 40, 42, 42) for back, pm, k1 (raglan st), pm, k10 for sleeve, pm, k1 (raglan st), pm, k34 (38, 38, 40, 42, 42) for front.

Inc rnd *K1 (raglan st), sl m, M1 (see Glossary), knit to next m, M1, sl m; rep from *—8 sts inc'd; 1 each side of raglan sts.

Knit 1 rnd even. Rep the last 2 rnds 17 (20, 24, 28, 32, 37) more times, changing to longer cir needle when necessary—236 (268, 300, 336, 372, 412) sts: 4 raglan sts, 70 (80, 88, 98, 108, 118) sts each for front and back, and 46 (52, 60, 68, 76, 86) sts for each sleeve.

Divide for Body + Sleeves

Place sts of front, back, and right sleeve on separate lengths of waste yarn, adding the raglan sts to the sleeve sections—48 (54, 62, 70, 78, 88) sts rem on needle for left sleeve.

SLEEVES

Transfer left-sleeve sts to shortest cir needle. With RS facing, use the backward-loop method (see Glossary) to CO 1 st at underarm, pm for beg-of-rnd, CO 1 more st, knit to end—50 (56, 64, 72, 80, 90) sts. Join for working in rnds. Work even in St st (knit every rnd) for 15 rnds.

Dec rnd K2tog, knit to last 2 sts, ssk—2 sts dec'd.

Work 7 rnds even. Changing to dpn when necessary, rep the last 8 rnds 4 (4, 4, 5, 5, 5) more times—40 (46, 54, 60, 68, 78) sts rem. Work even in St st until sleeve measures 9 (9, 10, 10, 11, 11)" (23 [23, 25.5, 25.5, 28, 28] cm) from underarm. BO all sts.

BODY

Place front and back sts on longest cir needle. Join yarn at left underarm, k 70 (80, 88, 98, 108, 118) front sts, pick up and knit 2 sts in gap at right underarm, k70 (80, 88, 98, 108, 118) back sts, pick up and knit 1 st in gap at left underarm, pm for beg of rnd, then pick up and knit 1 more st in the same gap—144 (164, 180, 200, 220, 240) sts total. Join for working in rnds and work even in St st until body measures 5 (5, 6, 6½, 7, 7½)" (12.5 [12.5, 15, 16.5, 18, 19] cm) from underarm.

Shape Waist

Set-up rnd *K14 (14, 15, 15, 16, 16), ssk, pm, k40 (50, 56, 66, 74, 84), pm, k2tog, k14 (14, 15, 15, 16, 16); rep from * once—4 sts dec'd; 2 sts each on front and back. Work 3 rnds even.

Dec rnd Knit to 2 sts before m, ssk, sl m, knit to next m, sl m, k2tog, knit to 2 sts before m, ssk, sl m, knit to next m, sl m, k2tog, knit to end—4 sts dec'd.

Work 3 rnds even. Rep the last 4 rnds 2 (2, 2, 3, 3, 3) more times—128 (148, 164, 180, 200, 220) sts rem. Work 4 (4, 4, 6, 6, 6) rnds even.

Inc rnd Knit to m, M1, sl m, knit to next m, sl m, M1, knit to m, M1, sl m, knit to next m, sl m, M1, knit to end —4 sts inc'd.

Work 3 rnds even. Rep the last 4 rnds 3 (3, 3, 4, 4, 4) more times—144 (164, 180, 200, 220, 240) sts. Work even until piece measures 15¾ (15¾, 15¾, 15½, 15½, 15)" (40 [40, 40, 39.5, 39.5, 38] cm) from underarm. Loosely BO all sts.

FINISHING

Weave in loose ends. Wash and block to measurements.

DEBBIE O'NEILL

was selected to be the featured designer for the Winter/Spring 2011 issue. She designs prolifically for publishers and yarn companies—a ubiquity stemming from her simple and appealing aesthetic, application of interesting stitch patterns to basic knits, and eye for fit. Her designs have been prevalent in *Knitscene* and always prove popular. Debbie blogs at nuttycreations .wordpress.com.

Originally published in Winter/Spring 2010

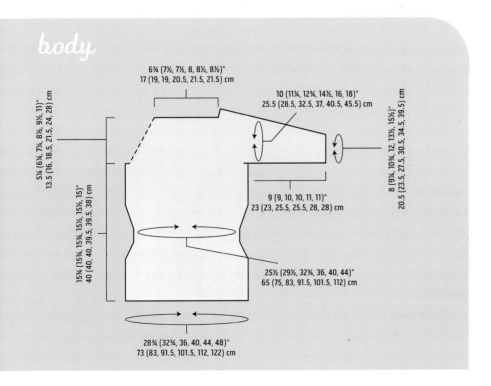

body

6¾ (7½, 7½, 8, 8½, 8½)"
17 (19, 19, 20.5, 21.5, 21.5) cm

10 (11¼, 12¾, 14½, 16, 18)"
25.5 (28.5, 32.5, 37, 40.5, 45.5) cm

5¼ (6¼, 7¼, 8½, 9¼, 11)"
13.5 (16, 18.5, 21.5, 24, 28) cm

8 (9¼, 10¾, 12, 13¾, 15½)"
20.5 (23.5, 27.5, 30.5, 34.5, 39.5) cm

9 (9, 10, 10, 11, 11)"
23 (23, 25.5, 25.5, 28, 28) cm

15¾ (15¾, 15¾, 15½, 15½, 15)"
40 (40, 40, 39.5, 39.5, 38) cm

25½ (29½, 32¾, 36, 40, 44)"
65 (75, 83, 91.5, 101.5, 112) cm

28¾ (32½, 36, 40, 44, 48)"
73 (83, 91.5, 101.5, 112, 122) cm

Fetching top-down socks feature an inventive cable design that spirals around the leg and foot. The visually spare design allows for use of handpainted and variegated yarns, but for print photography, solids show off stitches best—hence the classic camel here. The foot length can be adjusted for custom fit.

designed by **STAR ATHENA**

freshman cable socks

FINISHED SIZE
About 7" (18 cm) foot circumference and 9" (23 cm) long from tip of toe to back of heel. To fit women's U.S. shoe sizes 7 to 9 with adjustable foot length.

YARN
Fingering weight (#1 Super Fine).

SHOWN HERE Lorna's Laces Shepherd Sock (80% superwash wool, 20% nylon; 215 yd [197 m]/57 g): chino (tan), 2 skeins.

NEEDLES
Size U.S. 1 (2.25 mm): set of double-pointed (dpn) or 32" (81.5 cm) circular (cir) for magic-loop method.

Adjust needle size if necessary to obtain the correct gauge.

NOTIONS
Markers (m); cable needle (cn); tapestry needle.

GAUGE
32 sts and 48 rows = 4" (10 cm) in St st, worked in rnds.

NOTES
● These socks are worked from the top down.

● The spiraling cable effect is created by alternating Right Spiral and Left Spiral charts.

FIRST SOCK

Cuff

CO 60 sts. Arrange sts on dpn or cir needle as desired, place marker (pm), and join for working in rnds, being careful not to twist sts.

Set-up rnd P1, *k4, p2; rep from * to last 5 sts, k4, p1.

Work the sts as they appear (knit the knits and purl the purls) for 5 more rnds.

Leg

Set-up rnd Work Row 1 of Left Spiral chart over 30 sts, work Row 1 of Right Spiral chart over rem 30 sts.

Work even as established until Row 30 of charts has been completed.

Next rnd Work Row 1 of Right Spiral chart over 30 sts, work Row 1 of Left Spiral chart over rem 30 sts.

Work even as established until Row 30 of charts has been completed.

Next rnd Work Row 1 of Left Spiral chart over 30 sts, work Row 1 of Right Spiral chart over 30 sts.

Work even in patt for 4 more rnds—65 pattern rnds total; piece measures about 6" (15 cm) from CO edge.

Heel Flap

The heel flap is worked back and forth over 30 sts; the rem 30 sts will be worked later for the instep. The first st of every row is slipped and is counted as the first st of the chart.

☐ k on RS, p on WS

• p on RS, k on WS

sl 2 sts onto cn, hold in back, k2, k2 from cn

sl 2 sts onto cn, hold in front, k2, k2 from cn

LEFT SPIRAL

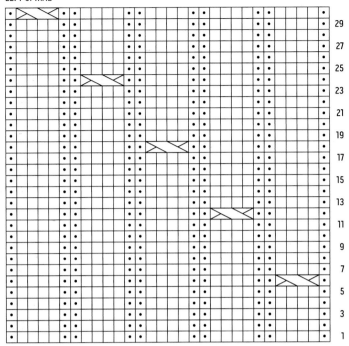

RIGHT SPIRAL

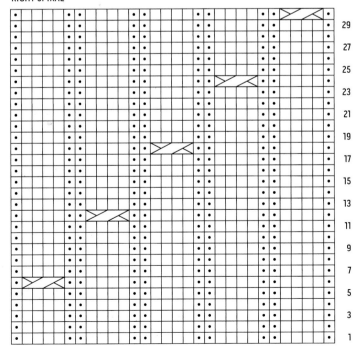

Row 1 (RS) Sl 1, work Row 6 of Left Spiral chart over 29 sts, turn.

Row 2 (WS) Sl 1, work Row 7 of Left Spiral chart over 29 sts, turn.

Cont in patt as established for 28 more rows, ending with Row 5 of charts.

Turn Heel

Work 30 heel sts in short-rows as foll:

Row 1 (RS) K18, ssk, k1, turn—29 sts rem.

Row 2 (WS) Sl 1, p7, p2tog, p1, turn—28 sts rem.

Row 3 Sl 1, k8, ssk, k1, turn—27 sts rem.

Row 4 Sl 1, p9, p2tog, p1, turn—26 sts rem.

Row 5 Sl 1, k10, ssk, k1, turn—25 sts rem.

Row 6 Sl 1, p11, p2tog, p1, turn—24 sts rem.

Row 7 Sl 1, k12, ssk, k1, turn—23 sts rem.

Row 8 Sl 1, p13 p2tog, p1, turn—22 sts rem.

Row 9 Sl 1, k14, ssk, k1, turn—21 sts rem.

Row 10 Sl 1, p15, p2tog, p1, turn—20 sts rem.

Row 11 Sl 1, k16, ssk, turn—19 sts rem.

Row 12 Sl 1, p16, p2tog, turn—18 sts rem.

Row 13 K18.

Gussets

Set-up rnd Pick up and knit 15 sts evenly spaced along slip st edge of heel flap, then 1 more st between heel flap and instep, pm, work Row 6 of Right Spiral chart across 30 instep sts, pm, pick up and knit 1 st between instep and heel flap, then 15 more sts along edge of heel flap—80 sts total. Join for working in rnds.

Rnd 1 K18, p13, k2tog, p1, sl m, work Row 7 of Right Spiral chart, sl m, p1, ssk, p13—78 sts rem.

Rnd 2 and all even-numbered rnds Knit to 1 st before m, p1, work next row of Right Spiral chart, p1, knit to end.

Rnd 3 Knit to 3 sts before m, k2tog, p1, work next row of Right Spiral chart, p1, ssk, knit to end—2 sts dec'd.

Rep Rnds 2 and 3 seven more times—62 sts rem.

Next rnd Knit to 1 st before m, p1, remove m, work next row of Right Spiral chart, remove m, p1, pm for new beg of rnd.

Foot

Rnd 1 K30, p1, work next rnd of Right Spiral chart, p1.

Cont in patt (alternating Left Spiral chart and Right Spiral chart every 30 rnds) until foot measures 7¾" (19.5 cm) from back of heel, or about 1¼" (3.2 cm) less than desired total length.

Toe

Set-up rnd K30, pm, k1, ssk, work in patt to last 3 sts, k2tog, k1—60 sts rem.

Rnd 1 Work even in patt.

Rnd 2 *K1, ssk, work in patt to 3 sts before m, k2tog, k1; rep from * once more—4 sts dec'd.

Rnd 3 Work even in patt.

Rep Rnds 2 and 3 six more times—32 sts rem.

Next rnd *K1, ssk, knit to 3 sts before m, k2tog, k1; rep from * once more—4 sts dec'd.

Rep last rnd 2 more times—20 sts rem. Arrange sts so there are 10 sts each on 2 needles. Break yarn, leaving a 12" (30.5 cm) tail. Thread tail on a tapestry needle and use the Kitchener st (see Glossary) to graft rem sts tog.

SECOND SOCK

Work as for first sock, substituting Right Spiral chart for Left Spiral chart and substituting Left Spiral chart for Right Spiral chart.

FINISHING

Weave in loose ends. Block as desired.

See page 54 for more information on designer **STAR ATHENA.**

Originally published in Fall 2009

star athena

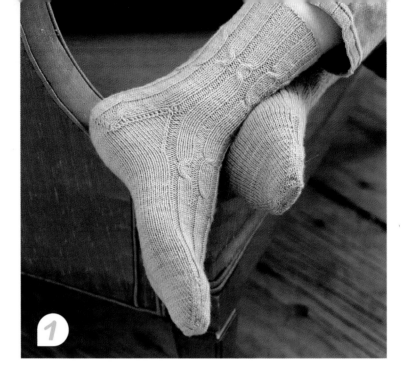

Star Athena is an artist, spinner, crocheter, and knit designer who lives along the river's edge in Portland, Oregon. She's currently hard at work producing designs for her monthly pattern club, Socks for All Seasons. The publishing schedule keeps her working on design every day—"No matter how busy the day is, I always dedicate a little time to daydreaming," she muses.

This propensity for daydream is not purely quixotic—Star is a problem-solver when it comes to design. "Usually I start with something conceptual and silly. Then I sketch it out and think about stitches that help translate the idea. As I work the pattern, it evolves on the needles. I think of the pattern as a puzzle. I have some theme in mind, but to get there technically, it involves a great deal of creativity (and math). The concept often changes a lot from idea to final sample, so I have to be careful about taking detailed notes marking the journey."

You get a glimpse of this journey from the Kimono Socks (page 56), which Star submitted to *Knitscene*

in response to our call for Global Knits. She details her process: "The Kimono Socks were inspired by the simple lines and geometry of a traditional kimono. I played around with wrapping and layering fabric around the cuff of a sock when it hit me to try stitch patterns that simulate a wrap without adding the extra bulk. I sketched a few ideas of what a kimono might look like wrapped around a foot and started to get really excited. The lines gave the socks interest from every angle."

Just like the Kimono Socks, the Freshman Cable Socks (page 50) feature mirror-image symmetry across right and left socks, which Star hopes will defer the dreaded second-sock syndrome.

When she's not designing, Star spends time making music, solving non-knitting puzzles, and exploring the Pacific Northwest. Or hanging out at Twisted, her favorite LYS.

Look for more on socks and life from Star at keeponknittinginthefreeworld.com.

KATHRYN MARTIN

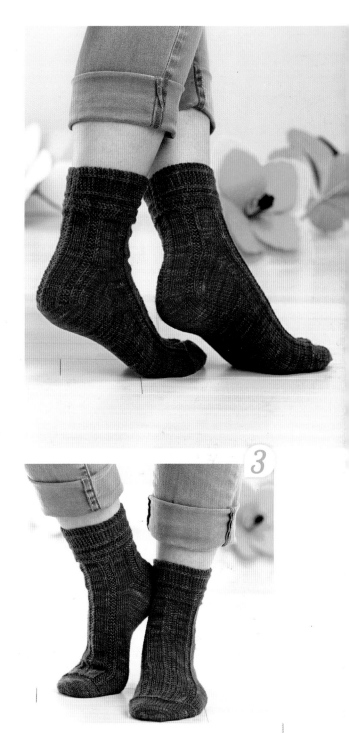

1. Freshman Cable Socks as shown on page 50. **2.** Star plays with three-color brioche in the subtly stunning **Pizzicato Scarf** (*Interweave Knits*, Fall 2010).
3. In the **Muscadine Socks** (*Sockupied*, Spring 2011), Star works from the toe up, then turns sideways to work the cuff.

Eyelet columns wrap and traverse these mirror-image socks, mimicking the surplice angles of kimonos. Little cords tie and knot to finish the effect. Star designed this pair in response to our call for "global knits" in the Fall 2008 issue. Just as for her Freshman Cable Socks on page 50, the non-intricate patterning makes this design ideal for multicolored yarns. *designed by* **STAR ATHENA**

kimono socks

FINISHED SIZE
About 7¼" (18.5 cm) foot circumference and 8½" (21.5 cm) long. To fit women's U.S. shoe sizes 7 to 9, with adjustable foot length.

YARN
Sportweight (#2 Fine).

SHOWN HERE Louet Gems Sport (100% superwash merino; 225 yd [206 m]/ 100 g): ginger, 2 skeins.

NEEDLES
Size U.S. 2 (2.75 mm): set of 4 double-pointed (dpn).

Adjust needle size if necessary to obtain the correct gauge.

NOTIONS
Markers (m); tapestry needle.

GAUGE
29 sts and 39 rows = 4" (10 cm) in St st, worked in rnds.

stitch guide

TWISTED RIB (multiple of 2 sts)
Rnd 1 *K1tbl, p1; rep from *.
Rep Rnd 1 for pattern.

MAKE TIE (MT)
Turn work, use the purled method (see Glossary) to CO 18 sts, BO these 18 sts pwise, sl last st on right needle tip to left needle tip, then turn work again.

SOCK

Cuff

CO 52 sts. Divide sts evenly on 3 dpn, place marker (pm), and join for working in rnds, being careful not to twist sts. Work in twisted rib (see Stitch Guide) for 1" (2.5 cm).

Left Leg

Rnd 1 Yo, pm, ssk, [k23, k2tog, pm, yo] 2 times.

Rnd 2 Knit.

Rnd 3 Knit to m, yo, slip marker (sl m), ssk, [knit to 2 sts before m, k2tog, sl m, yo] 2 times, knit to end of rnd.

Rnds 4–6 Rep Rnds 2 and 3 once more, then knit 1 rnd.

Rnd 7 Knit to m, yo, sl m, ssk, knit to 4 sts before m, MT (see Stitch Guide), [knit to 2 sts before m, k2tog, sl m, yo] 2 times, knit to end of rnd.

Rnd 8–10 Knit 1 rnd, rep Rnd 3 once, knit 1 rnd.

Rnd 11 Knit to m, yo, sl m, ssk, knit to 2 sts before m, k2tog, sl m, yo, k1, MT, knit to 2 sts before m, k2tog, sl m, yo, knit to end of rnd.

Rnds 12–24 [Knit 1 rnd, rep Rnd 3] 2 times, then knit 1 rnd, then rep Rnds 7–11 once, then knit 1 rnd, rep Rnd 3, knit 1 rnd.

Rnd 25 Knit to m, yo, sl m, sl 1, k2tog, psso, remove m, yo, knit to 2 sts before m, k2tog, sl m, yo, knit to end of rnd.

Rnd 26 Knit.

Rnd 27 Knit to m, yo, sl m, ssk, knit to 2 sts before m, k2tog, sl m, yo, knit to end of rnd.

Rnds 28–48 Rep the last 2 rnds 10 times, then knit 1 rnd.

Rnd 49 Knit to m, remove m, yo, ssk, k2tog, remove m, yo, knit to end of rnd, remove m.

Proceed to Heel.

Right Leg

Rnd 1 Yo, pm, ssk, k23, k2tog, pm, yo, M1 (see Glossary), pm, ssk, k23.

Rnd 2 Knit.

Rnd 3 Knit to m, yo, sl m, ssk, knit to 2 sts before m, k2tog, sl m, yo, knit to m, yo, sl m, ssk, knit to end of rnd.

Rnds 4–6 Rep Rnds 2 and 3 once more, then knit 1 rnd.

Rnd 7 Knit to m, yo, sl m, ssk, k2, MT, knit to 2 sts before m, k2tog, sl m, yo, knit to m, yo, sl m, ssk, knit to end of rnd.

Rnds 8–10 Knit 1 rnd, rep Rnd 3, knit 1 rnd.

Rnd 11 Knit to 2 sts before m, MT, k2, yo, sl m, ssk, knit to 2 sts before m, k2tog, sl m, yo, knit to m, yo, sl m, ssk, knit to end of rnd.

Rnds 12–24 [Knit 1 rnd, rep Rnd 3] 2 times, then knit 1 rnd, then rep Rnds 7–11 once, then knit 1 rnd, rep Rnd 3 once, knit 1 rnd.

Rnd 25 Knit to m, remove m, yo, ssk, sl st back to left needle, k2tog, sl m, yo, knit to m, yo, sl m, ssk, knit to end of rnd.

Rnd 26 Knit.

Rnd 27 Knit to 2 sts before m, k2tog, sl m, yo, knit to m, yo, sl m, ssk, knit to end of rnd.

Rnds 28–48 Rep the last 2 rnds 10 times, then knit 1 rnd.

Rnd 49 K1, k2tog, remove m, yo, knit to m, remove m, yo, ssk (the last st of this rnd and first st of next rnd), sl st back to left needle, remove m.

Heel

The heel flap is worked back and forth over the last 26 sts of the rnd; the first 26 sts will be worked later for instep.

Set-up row Turn work and, with WS facing, sl 1, p25.

Row 1 (RS) Sl 1, k25.

Row 2 (WS) Sl 1, p25.

Rep these 2 rows 10 more times—22 rows total.

Turn Heel

Work short-rows as foll:

Row 1 (RS) Sl 1, k14, ssk, k1, turn.

Row 2 (WS) Sl 1, p5, p2tog, p1, turn.

Row 3 Sl 1, knit to 1 st before gap, ssk, k1, turn.

Row 4 Sl 1, purl to 1 st before gap, p2tog, p1, turn.

Rep the last 2 rows 3 more times—16 sts rem. K16 heel sts.

Gussets + Foot

Set-up rnd With an empty needle (Needle 1), pick up and knit 12 sts along sl st edge of heel flap, then 1 st between heel flap and instep; with an empty needle (Needle 2), k26 instep sts; with an empty needle (Needle 3), pick up and knit 1 st between instep and heel flap, then 12 sts along other sl st edge of heel flap, then knit the first 8 heel sts, pm for beg of rnd, then sl rem 8 heel sts from heel needle onto Needle 1—68 sts total: 21 sts on Needle 1, 26 instep sts on Needle 2, and 21 sts on Needle 3.

Continue for left or right foot as follows.

LEFT FOOT

Rnd 1 On Needle 1, knit to last 3 sts, k2tog, k1; on Needle 2, k24, k2tog, pm, yo; on Needle 3, k1, ssk, knit to end—66 sts rem.

Rnd 2 Knit.

Rnd 3 On Needle 1, knit to last 3 sts, k2tog, k1; on Needle 2, knit to 2 sts before m, k2tog, sl m, yo, knit to end of needle; on Needle 3, k1, ssk, knit to end—2 sts dec'd.

Rep the last 2 rnds 5 more times, then work Rnd 2 once again—54 sts rem.

Next rnd On Needle 1, knit to last 3 sts, k2tog, k1; on Needle 2, yo, pm, ssk, knit to 2 sts before m, k2tog, sl m, yo, knit to end of needle; on Needle 3, k1, ssk, knit to end—52 sts rem: 13 sts on Needle 1, 26 sts on Needle 2, and 13 sts on Needle 3.

Knit 1 rnd.

Next rnd Knit to m, yo, sl m, ssk, knit to 2 sts before m, k2tog, sl m, yo, knit to end of rnd.

Next rnd Knit.

Rep the last 2 rnds 6 more times.

Next rnd Knit to m, remove m, knit to 2 sts before m, k2tog, sl m, yo, knit to end of rnd. Next rnd: Knit.

Next rnd Knit to 2 sts before m, k2tog, sl m, yo, knit to end of rnd.

Rep the last 2 rnds 8 more times. Knit 1 rnd, removing m.

Proceed to Toe.

RIGHT FOOT

Rnd 1 On Needle 1, knit to last 3 sts, k2tog, k1; on Needle 2, yo, pm, ssk, knit to end of needle; on Needle 3, k1, ssk, knit to end—66 sts rem.

Rnd 2 Knit.

Rnd 3 On Needle 1, knit to last 3 sts, k2tog, k1; on Needle 2, knit to m, yo, sl m, ssk, knit to end of needle; on Needle 3, k1, ssk, knit to end—2 sts dec'd.

Rep the last 2 rnds 5 more times, then work Rnd 2 once again—54 sts rem.

Next rnd On Needle 1, knit to last 3 sts, k2tog, k1; on Needle 2, knit to m, yo, sl m, ssk, knit to last 2 sts, k2tog, pm, yo; on Needle 3: k1, ssk, knit to end—52 sts rem: 13 sts on Needle 1, 26 sts on Needle 2, and 13 sts on Needle 3.

Knit 1 rnd.

Next rnd Knit to m, yo, sl m, ssk, knit to 2 sts before m, k2tog, sl m, yo, knit to end of rnd.

Next rnd Knit.

Rep the last 2 rnds 6 more times.

Next rnd Knit to m, yo, sl m, ssk, knit to m, remove m, knit to end of rnd.

Next rnd Knit.

Next rnd Knit to m, yo, sl m, ssk, knit to end of rnd.

Rep the last 2 rnds 8 more times. Knit 1 rnd, removing m.

Toe

Rnd 1 On Needle 1, knit to last 3 sts, k2tog, k1; on Needle 2, k1, ssk, knit to last 3 sts, k2tog, k1; on Needle 3, k1, ssk, knit to end—4 sts dec'd.

Rnd 2 Knit.

Rep the last 2 rnds 7 more times —20 sts rem. K5 from Needle 1 onto Needle 3—10 sts each on 2 needles. Break yarn, leaving a 20" (51 cm) tail.

FINISHING

Thread tail on a tapestry needle and use the Kitchener st (see page 137) to graft rem sts tog. Weave in loose ends. Block as desired.

See page 54 for more information on designer **STAR ATHENA**.

Originally published in Fall 2008

Varying texture patterns, asymmetry, and clean edges make a great casual jacket. Norah Gaughan designed this cardigan for men, but we found that women love it for themselves—in fact, we used a photo of the sample on a female model for the cover of the Spring 2007 issue. Roll up the cuffs and you're good to go.

designed by **NORAH GAUGHAN**

kenobi jacket

FINISHED SIZE
About 42 (46, 50, 54)"
(106.5 [117, 127, 137] cm)
chest circumference, closed.
Sweater shown measures
42" (106.5 cm).

YARN
Worsted weight
(#4 Medium).

SHOWN HERE Berroco Ultra
Alpaca (50% alpaca, 50%
wool; 215 yd [198 m]/
100 g): #14 brown, 11
(12 13, 14) skeins.

NEEDLES
Sizes U.S. 8 (5 mm)
and 10 (6 mm).

*Adjust needle size if
necessary to obtain the
correct gauge.*

NOTIONS
Tapestry needle.

GAUGE
14 sts and 21 rows = 4"
(10 cm) in moss st with
larger needles and yarn
doubled.

NOTES
◆ Yarn is held doubled
throughout.

◆ The patterning of
the fronts and back is
deliberately asymmetrical.

stitch guide

MOSS STITCH (multiple of 2 sts)

Rows 1 and 2 (RS and WS) *P1, k1; rep from *.

Rows 3 and 4 (RS and WS) *K1, p1; rep from *.

Rep Rows 1–4 for pattern.

1X1 RIB (multiple of 2 sts)

All Rows *K1, p1; rep from *.

3X3 RIB (multiple of 6 sts)

All Rows *K3, p3; rep from * to end.

BACK

With yarn doubled and larger needles, CO 80 (88, 96, 104) sts.

Set-up row (RS) Work 16 (18, 20, 22) sts in moss st (see Stitch Guide), 16 (18, 20, 22) sts in rev St st (purl RS rows; knit WS rows), 8 sts in 1×1 rib (see Stitch Guide), 10 (12, 14, 16) sts in moss st, 10 sts in rev St st, 12 sts in 3×3 rib (see Stitch Guide), and rem 8 (10, 12, 14) sts in St st (knit RS rows; purl WS rows).

Next row (WS) Work 8 (10, 12, 14) sts in St st, 12 sts in 3×3 rib, 10 sts in rev St st, 10 (12, 14,16) sts in moss st, 8 sts in 1×1 rib, 16 (18, 20, 22) sts in rev St st, and rem 16 (18, 20, 22) sts in moss st.

Rep the last 2 rows until piece measures 19" (48.5 cm) from CO, ending with a WS row.

Shape Armholes

BO 3 sts at beg of next 2 rows, then BO 2 sts at beg of next 0 (2, 4, 6) rows, then BO 1 st at beg of next 4 rows—70 (74, 78, 82) sts rem. Work even in patt until armholes measure 8½ (9, 9½, 10)" (21.5 [23, 24, 25.5] cm), ending with a WS row.

Shape Shoulders

BO 8 (9, 8, 9) sts at beg of next 2 rows, then BO 8 sts at beg of next 4 rows—22 (24, 30, 32) sts rem. BO all sts.

LEFT FRONT

With yarn doubled and larger needles, CO 43 (47, 51, 55) sts.

Set-up row (RS) Work 16 (18, 20, 22) sts in moss st, 16 (18, 20, 22) sts in rev St st, 8 sts in 1×1 rib, then k3.

Next row (WS) With yarn held in front (wyf), sl 3 sts, work next 8 sts in 1×1 rib, 16 (18, 20, 22) sts in rev St st, and rem 16 (18, 20, 22) sts in moss st.

Rep the last 2 rows until piece measures 19" (48.5 cm) from CO, ending with a WS row.

Shape Armhole

BO 3 sts at beg of next RS row, then BO 2 sts at beg of next 0 (1, 2, 3) RS row(s), then BO 1 st at beg of next 2 RS rows—38 (40, 42, 44) sts rem. Work even in patt until armhole measures 7½ (8, 8½, 9)" (19 [20.5, 21.5, 23] cm), ending with a RS row.

Shape Neck + Shoulder

Note Shoulder shaping begs as neck shaping is worked; read all the way through the next section before proceeding.

Cont in patt, BO 4 (5, 6, 7) sts at beg of next WS row, then BO 3 sts at beg of foll

WS row, then BO 2 sts at beg of foll 3 WS rows, then BO 1 st at beg of foll WS row. *At the same time* when armhole measures 8½ (9, 9½, 10)" (21.5 [23, 24, 25.5] cm), shape shoulder as foll: BO 8 (9, 8, 9) sts at beg of next RS row, then BO 8 (8, 9, 9) sts at beg of foll 2 RS rows—no sts rem.

RIGHT FRONT

With yarn doubled and larger needles, CO 43 (47, 51, 55) sts.

Set-up row (RS) Sl 3 sts with yarn held in back (wyb), work 10 (12, 14, 16) sts in moss st, 10 sts in rev St st, 12 sts in 3×3 rib, and rem 8 (10, 12, 14) sts in St st.

Next row (WS) Work 8 (10, 12, 14) sts in St st, 12 sts in 3×3 rib, 10 sts in rev St st, 10 (12, 14, 16) sts in moss st, then p3.

Rep the last 2 rows until piece measures 19" (48.5 cm) from CO, ending with a RS row.

Shape Armhole

BO 3 sts at beg of next WS row, then BO 2 sts at beg of next 0 (1, 2, 3) WS row(s), then BO 1 st at beg of next 2 WS rows—38 (40, 42, 44) sts rem. Work even in patt until armhole measures 7½ (8, 8½, 9)" (19 [20.5, 21.5, 23] cm), ending with a WS row.

Shape Neck + Shoulder

Note Shoulder shaping begs as neck shaping is worked.

Cont in patt, BO 4 (5, 6, 7) sts at beg of next RS row, then BO 3 sts at beg of foll RS row, then BO 2 sts at beg of foll 3 RS rows, then BO 1 st at beg of foll RS row.

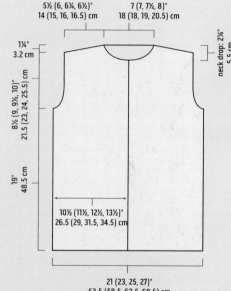

front & back

5½ (6, 6¼, 6½)"
14 (15, 16, 16.5) cm

7 (7, 7½, 8)"
18 (18, 19, 20.5) cm

1¼"
3.2 cm

neck drop: 2¼"
5.5 cm

8½ (9, 9½, 10)"
21.5 (23, 24, 25.5) cm

19"
48.5 cm

10½ (11½, 12½, 13½)"
26.5 (29, 31.5, 34.5) cm

21 (23, 25, 27)"
53.5 (58.5, 63.5, 68.5) cm

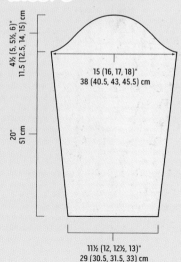

sleeve

4½ (5, 5½, 6)"
11.5 (12.5, 14, 15) cm

15 (16, 17, 18)"
38 (40.5, 43, 45.5) cm

20"
51 cm

11½ (12, 12½, 13)"
29 (30.5, 31.5, 33) cm

At the same time when armhole measures 8½ (9, 9½, 10)" (21.5 [23, 24, 25.5] cm), shape shoulder as foll: BO 8 (9, 8, 9) sts at beg of next WS row, then BO 8 (8, 9, 9) sts at beg of foll 2 WS rows—no sts rem.

SLEEVES

With yarn doubled and larger needles, CO 42 (44, 46, 48) sts.

Set-up row (RS) Work 13 (14, 15, 16) sts in St st, 8 sts in 1×1 rib, 9 (10, 11, 12) sts in rev St st, and rem 12 sts in moss st.

Next row (WS) Work 12 sts in moss st, 9 (10, 11, 12) sts in rev St st, 8 sts in 1×1 rib, and rem 13 (14, 15, 16) sts in St st.

Rep the last 2 rows until piece measures 2" (5 cm) from CO. Inc 1 st at each end of needle on next row, then on every 10th row 5 (6, 6, 7) more times, working new sts into patt—54 (58, 60, 64) sts. Work even in patt until piece measures 20" (51 cm) from CO.

Shape Cap

BO 3 sts at beg of next 2 rows, then BO 2 sts at beg of foll 2 rows—44 (48, 50, 54) sts rem.

Dec row K1, k2tog, work in patt to last 3 sts, ssk, k1—2 sts dec'd.

Rep dec row every RS row 7 (8, 9, 10) more times—28 (30, 30, 32) sts rem. BO 2 sts at beg of next 2 rows, then BO 3 sts at beg of foll 2 rows—18 (20, 20, 22) sts rem. BO all sts.

FINISHING

Block pieces to measurements.

Seams

With yarn threaded on a tapestry needle, sew fronts to back at shoulders. Sew sleeve caps into armholes. Sew sleeve and side seams.

Collar

With RS facing, smaller needle, and yarn doubled, pick up and knit 70 (74, 78, 82) sts evenly spaced around neck opening.

Next row (WS) *P2, k2; rep from * to last 2 sts, p2.

Next row (RS) *K2, p2; rep from * to last 2 sts, k2.

Rep the last 2 rows until collar measures 3" (7.5 cm). BO all sts.

Weave in loose ends.

NORAH GAUGHAN is the author of *Knitting Nature* (Stewart, Tabori & Chang, 2006). She is a designer with Berroco Yarns, for whom she's developed a beautiful line of eponymous pattern booklets. She also blogs for the company at blog.berroco.com.

Originally published in Spring 2007

A lofty alpaca blend drapes beautifully in this top-down seamless raglan. Its heathered coloring deepens the richness of the cable—an opulent stitch that adorns the center front panel. Wendy Bernard worked up this design in answer to our call for medieval-inspired projects. The flared cuff alludes to the lacy cuffs of medieval and rococo blouses, a reference echoed by the squared neckline.

designed by **WENDY BERNARD**

opulent raglan

FINISHED SIZE
32¼ (34¾, 36½, 40¾, 44, 48¼, 50¾)" (82 [88.5, 92.5, 103.5, 112, 122.5, 129] cm) bust circumference. Sweater shown measures 34¾" (88.5 cm).

YARN
Worsted weight
(#4 Medium).

SHOWN HERE GGH Cumba (47% wool, 28% alpaca, 25% acrylic; 162 yd [150 m]/50 g): #79393 taupe, 5 (5, 6, 7, 9, 9, 10) balls.

NEEDLES
Size U.S. 6 (4 mm): 29" or longer circular (cir) and set of double-pointed (dpn). Size U.S. 5 (3.5 mm): 24" or longer cir.

Adjust needle size if necessary to obtain the correct gauge.

NOTIONS
Markers (m); cable needle (cn); waste yarn; tapestry needle.

GAUGE
19 sts and 22 rows = 4" (10 cm) in St st on larger needles.

NOTES
● This sweater is worked from the top down.

● Before joining front below neckline, garment is worked flat in rows; after joining back and front, the body is worked in the round.

stitch guide

7/6 LEFT CROSS (LC)
Sl 6 sts onto cn and hold in front, k6, p1, k6 from cn.

RIGHT TWIST (RT)
Knit 2nd st on left needle but do not drop st from needle, knit first st on left needle, then drop both sts from needle.

OPULENT CABLE (worked over 13 sts)
Rnds 1, 3, 5, 7, 9, 11, 15, and 17 K6, p1, k6.
Even-numbered Rnds 2–20 Work sts as they appear.
Rnds 13 and 19 7/6 LC (see above).
Rep Rnds 1–20 for pattern.

EASY BRAID (worked over 2 sts)
Rnd 1 RT (see above).
Rnd 2 K2.
Rep these 2 rows for pattern.

YOKE

With larger cir needle, CO 2 (2, 2, 2, 4, 6, 6) sts for one front, place marker (pm), then CO 2 (2, 2, 2, 4, 4, 4) sts for sleeve, pm, then CO 26 (26, 28, 30, 36, 40, 42) sts for back, pm, the CO 2 (2, 2, 2, 4, 4, 4) sts for other sleeve, pm, then CO 2 (2, 2, 2, 4, 6, 6) sts for other front—34 (34, 36, 38, 52, 60, 62) sts total. Do not join.

Inc row (RS) Knit to m, sl m, k1f&b (see Glossary), [knit to 1 st before next m, k1f&b, sl m, k1f&b] 2 times, knit to 1 st before next m, k1f&b, sl m, knit to end—6 sts inc'd.

Purl 1 WS row. Rep the last 2 rows 5 (5, 5, 5, 3, 3, 3) more times—70 (70, 72, 74, 76, 84, 86) sts.

SHAPE NECK

Inc row (RS) [Knit to 1 st before next m, k1f&b, sl m, k1f&b] 4 times, knit to end—8 sts inc'd.

Purl 1 WS row. Rep the last 2 rows 11 (13, 13, 15, 17, 17, 17) more times—166 (182, 184, 202, 220, 228, 230) sts: 14 (16, 16, 18, 22, 24, 24) sts for each front, 38 (42, 42, 46, 48, 48, 48) sts for each sleeve, and 62 (66, 68, 74, 80, 84, 86) sts for back.

Work 1 WS row even.

Lower Body

Joining rnd With RS facing, knit across right front sts, remove m, place sleeve sts on waste yarn, remove m, use the backward-loop method (see Glossary) to CO 7 (8, 9, 11, 12, 15, 17) sts, pm for beg of rnd, CO 7 (8, 9, 11, 12, 15, 17) more sts, pm, work across back sts to m, remove m, place sleeve sts on waste yarn, CO 7 (8, 9, 11, 12, 15, 17) sts, sl m for "side seam," CO 7 (8, 9, 11, 12, 15, 17) more sts, work across left front sts, pm for cable panel, CO 35 (35, 37, 39, 37, 37, 39) sts for cable panel, pm, join for working in rnds—153 (165, 173, 193, 209, 229, 241) sts total.

Work sts on each side of cable panel in St st (knit all rnds) and work cable panel as foll:

Rnd 1 Knit to cable-panel m, p3, work Rnd 1 of easy braid (see Stitch Guide) over 2 sts, p2, work Rnd 1 of easy braid

body & sleeve

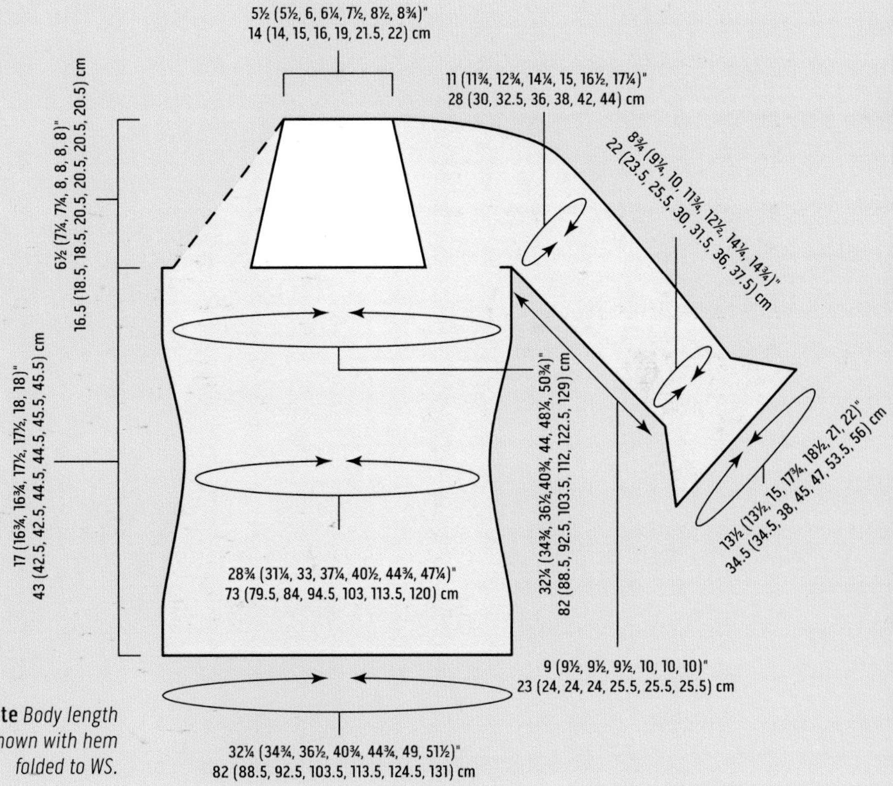

5½ (5½, 6, 6¼, 7½, 8½, 8¾)"
14 (14, 15, 16, 19, 21.5, 22) cm
11 (11¾, 12¾, 14¼, 15, 16½, 17¼)"
28 (30, 32.5, 36, 38, 42, 44) cm
8¾ (9¼, 10, 11¾, 12½, 14¼, 14¾)"
22 (23.5, 25.5, 30, 31.5, 36, 37.5) cm
6½ (7¼, 7¼, 8, 8, 8, 8)"
16.5 (18.5, 18.5, 20.5, 20.5, 20.5, 20.5) cm
17 (16¾, 16¾, 17½, 17½, 18, 18)"
43 (42.5, 42.5, 44.5, 44.5, 45.5, 45.5) cm
32¼ (34¾, 36½, 40¾, 44, 48¼, 50¾)"
82 (88.5, 92.5, 103.5, 112, 122.5, 129) cm
13½ (13½, 15, 17¾, 18½, 21, 22)"
34.5 (34.5, 38, 45, 47, 53.5, 56) cm
28¾ (31¼, 33, 37¼, 40½, 44¾, 47¼)"
73 (79.5, 84, 94.5, 103, 113.5, 120) cm
9 (9½, 9½, 9½, 10, 10, 10)"
23 (24, 24, 24, 25.5, 25.5, 25.5) cm
32¼ (34¾, 36½, 40¾, 44¾, 49, 51½)"
82 (88.5, 92.5, 103.5, 113.5, 124.5, 131) cm

Note *Body length shown with hem folded to WS.*

over 2 sts, p2 (2, 3, 4, 3, 3, 4), work Rnd 1 of opulent cable (see Stitch Guide) over 13 sts, p2 (2, 3, 4, 3, 3, 4), work Rnd 1 of easy braid over 2 sts, p2, work Rnd 1 of easy braid over 2 sts, p3, knit to end of rnd.

Work in established patt for 21 (19, 19, 23, 23, 27, 27) rnds.

SHAPE WAIST

Dec rnd K1, k2tog, work to 3 sts before next side m, ssk, k1, sl m, k1, k2tog, work to 3 sts before end-of-rnd m, ssk, k1—4 sts dec'd.

Cont in patt, rep dec rnd every 5th rnd 3 more times—137 (149, 157, 177, 193, 213, 225) sts rem. Work 5 rnds even.

Inc rnd K1, M1 (see Glossary), work to 1 st before next side m, M1, k1, sl m, k1, M1, work to 1 st before end-of-rnd m, M1, k1—4 sts inc'd.

Cont in patt, rep inc rnd every 5th rnd 3 (3, 3, 3, 4, 4, 4) more times—153 (165, 173, 193, 213, 233, 245) sts. Work even in patt until piece measures about 23½ (24, 24, 25½, 25½, 26, 26)" (59.5 [61, 61, 65, 65, 66, 66] cm) from back neck, ending with Rnd 6 or 18 of cable patt. Purl 1 rnd (turning rnd). Change to smaller needle and knit 6 rnds for hem. BO all sts.

SLEEVES

Place 38 (42, 42, 46, 48, 48, 48) held sleeve sts on dpn, join yarn, knit all sts, pick up and knit 7 (7, 9, 11, 12, 15, 17) sts to center of underarm CO, pm for beg of rnd, pick up and knit 7 (7, 9, 11, 12, 15, 17) more sts to end of underarm CO,

and join for working in rnds—52 (56, 60, 68, 72, 78, 82) sts total. Knit 2 rnds.

Dec rnd K1, k2tog, knit to 3 sts before end of rnd, ssk, k1—2 sts dec'd.

Work 7 (8, 8, 9, 9, 9) rnds even. Rep dec rnd every 8 (9, 9, 9, 10, 10, 10)th rnd 4 (5, 5, 5, 5, 4, 5) more times—42 (44, 48, 56, 60, 68, 70) sts rem. Work even until sleeve measures 9 (9½, 9½, 9½, 10, 10, 10)" (23 [24, 24, 24, 25.5, 25.5, 25.5] cm) from underarm.

CUFF

Inc 22 (20, 24, 28, 28, 32, 34) sts for your size as foll:

SIZE 32¼" (82 CM) ONLY
M1, *k2, M1; rep from * to end—64 sts.

**SIZES 34¾ (44, 48¼, 50¾)"
(88.5 [112, 122.5, 129] CM) ONLY**
K2, *k2, M1; rep from * to last 2 (2, 2, 0) sts, k2 (2, 2, 0)—64 (88, 100, 104) sts.

**SIZES 36½ (40¾)"
(92.5 [103.5] CM) ONLY**
*K2, M1; rep from * to end—72 (84) sts.

ALL SIZES
Rnd 1 *K2, p2; rep from *.

Rnd 2 *RT, p2; rep from *.

Rep Rnds 1 and 2 two more times.

Inc rnd *K2, p1, M1P (see Glossary), p1; rep from * to end—80 (80, 90, 105, 110, 125, 130) sts.

Rnd 3 *RT, p3; rep from *.

Rnd 4 *K2, p3; rep from *.

Rep Rnds 3 and 4 five more times. BO all sts in patt.

FINISHING

Neckband

With removable markers, mark left-most st and right-most st at corners of lower edge of front neckline. With smaller cir needle, RS facing, and beg at top of left sleeve, pick up and knit 2 (2, 2, 2, 4, 4, 4) sts along top of sleeve, 30 (34, 34, 38, 38, 38, 38) sts along left neck edge to left marked st, pm, 34 (34, 36, 38, 36, 36, 38) sts along front neck to right marked st, pm, 30 (34, 34, 38, 38, 38, 38) sts up right neck edge, 2 (2, 2, 2, 4, 4, 4) sts along top of right sleeve, and 26 (26, 28, 30, 36, 40, 42) sts along back neck—124 (132, 136, 148, 156, 160, 164) sts. Pm and join for working in rnds.

Dec rnd Work in k1, p1 rib to 2 sts before first neck m, sl 1, k1, psso, work in patt to next m, k2tog, work in patt to end—2 sts dec'd.

Rep dec rnd 2 more times. Loosely BO all sts in patt. Turn hem to WS along purl rnd and, with yarn threaded on a tapestry needle, tack in place.

Weave in loose ends. Block to measurements.

WENDY BERNARD
is a knitwear designer and blogger who lives in Southern California. She obsessively reads the *Farmer's Almanac* to see if and when she can wear her knits. Wendy is author of *Custom Knits* (Stewart, Tabori & Chang, 2008). See more at knitandtonic.net.

**Originally published
in Fall 2008**

A wide scarf earns its luxurious drape—
and wrapability—from columns of
dropped stitches. The openwork ladders
lend fluidity and interest to an otherwise
simple stockinette project. Braided fringe
finishes the luxe look.

designed by **KATIE HIMMELBERG**

phiaro scarf

FINISHED SIZE
About 22" (56 cm) wide and
90" (228.5 cm) long, including
fringe.

YARN
Worsted weight (#4 medium).

SHOWN HERE Southwest
Trading Company Oasis
(100% soy silk; 240 yd
[262 m]/100 g): #053
chocolate, 3 balls.

NEEDLES
Size U.S. 7 (4.5 mm): 16"
(40.5 cm) circular (cir).

*Adjust needle size if necessary
to obtain the correct gauge.*

NOTIONS
Marker (m); size H/8 (5 mm)
crochet hook; tapestry needle.

GAUGE
20 sts and 26 rnds = 4"
(10 cm) in St st worked in
rnds, after blocking.

NOTES
● This scarf is worked in the
round; stitches are dropped as
they are bound off to create
the dropped-stitch sections as
well as the fringe.

● The fringe is cut open during
finishing.

SCARF

CO 195 sts. Place marker (m) and join for working in rnds. Work in St st (knit every rnd) until piece measures 22" (56 cm) from CO.

Next rnd BO 5 sts, break yarn, leaving a 4" (10 cm) tail; drop next 5 sts and ravel them down to CO edge. *Using crochet hook, join yarn and BO next 5 sts, break yarn, leaving 4" tail (10 cm), drop next 5 sts and ravel them down to CO edge; rep from * to last 35 sts, join yarn, BO 5 sts, break yarn, drop next 30 sts for fringe.

FINISHING

Fold fringe section in half, matching the 5-st columns on each end. Cut fringe along the center. Weave in ends from BO. Braid fringe using 3 strands of yarn for each braid, making some 4-strand braids as necessary. Knot and trim ends. Steam-press gently to set sts.

KATIE HIMMELBERG

has worked on the *Knitscene* staff as both photostylist and style editor. She currently lives in Northern Colorado with her young family and blogs at katiehimmelberg .wordpress.com.

Originally published in Winter 07/Spring 08

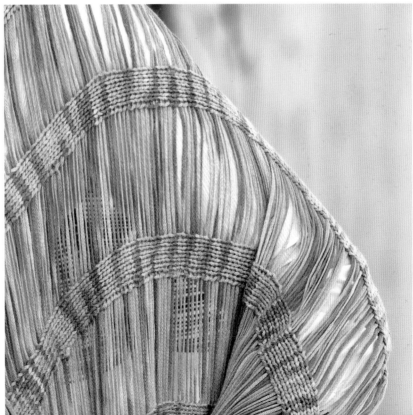

Cecily Glowik MacDonald worked long, ladylike mitts in a haloed alpaca that slides like silk over the hand. Lacy buttonloops close the long ribbed cuff—choose pearl, leather, or funky plastic buttons to create your own style.

designed by **CECILY GLOWIK MACDONALD**

michaelmas mitts

FINISHED SIZE
About 8" (20.5 cm) hand circumference and 13" (33 cm) long.

YARN
Worsted weight (#4 Medium).

SHOWN HERE Blue Sky Alpacas Suri Merino (60% alpaca, 40% merino; 164 yd [150 m]/100 g): #414 Sahara (beige), 2 skeins.

NEEDLES
Size U.S. 6 (4 mm).

Adjust needle size if necessary to obtain the correct gauge.

NOTIONS
Markers (m); tapestry needle; sixteen ½" (1.3 cm) buttons.

GAUGE
21 sts and 28 rows = 4" (10 cm) in St st.

NOTE
● The mitts are worked back and forth in rows, then seamed along the outside edge of the wrist and hand.

MITTS

CO 47 sts.

Wrist

Row 1 (RS) P2, *k1, sl 1 with yarn in back (wyb), k1, p2; rep from *.

Row 2 (WS) *K2, p3; rep from * to last 2 sts, k2.

Rep Rows 1 and 2 until piece measures 1½" (3.8 cm) from CO, ending with a WS row.

Dec row (RS) P2tog, *k1, sl 1 with yarn in front (wyf), k1, p2tog; rep from * to end—37 sts rem.

Row 1 (WS) K1, *p3, k1; rep from *.

Row 2 (RS) P1, *k1, sl 1 wyf, k1, p1; rep from *.

Rep the last 2 rows until piece measures 8" (20.5 cm) from CO, ending with a WS row.

Hand

Work 2 rows even in St st (knit RS rows; purl WS rows).

Next row (RS) Cont in St st, inc 10 sts evenly spaced—47 sts.

Work 2 rows even in St st, ending with a RS row.

THUMB GUSSET

With WS facing, p22, place m (pm), p3, pm, p22.

Inc row (RS) Knit to m, sl m, k1, work a left lifted inc (LLI; see Glossary), knit to 1 st before next m, work a right lifted inc (RLI; see Glossary), k1, sl m, knit to end of row—2 sts inc'd.

Next row (WS) Purl.

Rep the last 2 rows 6 more times, ending with a WS row—61 sts total: 17 sts between m. Work 2 rows even in St st.

Next row (RS) Knit to m, BO 17 sts, knit to end of row—44 sts rem.

Next row (WS) Purl, closing gap above thumbhole by pulling tightly on working yarn after passing the gap.

UPPER HAND

Work even in St st until piece measures 1½" (3.8 cm) from thumb gusset BO, ending with a WS row.

Next row (RS) Inc 3 sts evenly spaced—47 sts.

Row 1 (WS) *K2, p3; rep from * to last 2 sts, k2.

Row 2 (RS) P2, *k1, sl 1 wyb, k1, p2; rep from *.

Rep the last 2 rows for 1" (2.5 cm), ending with a WS row. BO all sts in patt, leaving a 15" (38 cm) tail for seaming.

FINISHING

Thread tail on a tapestry needle and sew hand closed from BO edge to beg of wrist rib.

Buttonband

With RS facing and beg at CO edge, pick up and knit 44 sts evenly spaced along left side to end of wrist rib.

Rows 1 and 3 (WS) K2, p40, k2.

Row 2 (RS) Knit.

With RS facing, BO all sts.

On second mitt, pick up sts for buttonband along right side of opening, from end of wrist rib to CO, and work as for first buttonband.

Buttonhole Band

CO 52 sts.

Row 1 (RS) K1, yo, *k5, pass the 2nd, 3rd, 4th, and 5th sts over the first st, yo; rep from * to last st, k1—23 sts rem.

Row 2 P1, *(p1, yo, k1tbl) in next st, p1; rep from * to end—45 sts.

Row 3 K2, k1tbl, *k3, k1tbl; rep from * to last 2 sts, k2.

Row 4 Purl.

BO all sts. Sew BO edge of buttonhole band to side of rib opening opposite buttonband.

Sew 8 buttons to each buttonband, opposite the first 8 holes between shells formed on buttonhole band. Weave in loose ends. Block as desired.

For more information on **CECILY GLOWIK MACDONALD**, see profile on page 82.

Originally published in Fall 2008

cecily glowik macdonald

INSPIRATION CAN come quickly and frenetically to Cecily Glowik MacDonald. "Just doing a stockinette swatch in a particular yarn can bring ideas, or seeing an interesting detail on a ready-to-wear garment . . . often right before I fall asleep I get a ton of ideas and have to get up and do quick sketches." "Constant brainstorming" is essential for this full-time freelancer, who's recently been self-publishing at the rate of three or more patterns a month, and whose Ravelry portfolio boasts more than 200 original designs.

Cecily has contributed to *Knitscene* with great frequency, which makes sense as her design philosophy coincides with ours: "I absolutely love the challenge of designing something that is attractive and fun to wear, yet super easy to knit." The Pinch Hat (page 84) demonstrates her ability to design simple but singular accessories, while the Michaelmas Mitts (page 78) show off her girly sensibility.

An oils painter who lived in a cramped apartment in Brooklyn, Cecily found herself unable to produce much art without an adequate studio. Luckily, a friend introduced her to knitting and she hasn't put the needles down since. After working as an in-house designer for Classic Elite Yarns for a few years in Massachusetts, Cecily and her husband relocated to Maine. There she coauthored the popular *New England Knits* (Interweave, 2010) with friend Melissa LaBarre. She continues to publish widely with yarn companies, magazines, and on her own site.

What's next for Cecily? "When I'm able to put down the knitting needles, I plan on taking a sewing class." Until then, the knitting keeps her busy at cecilyam .wordpress.com.

JOE COCA

1. Pebble Hoodie (*Knitscene* Winter 2007/Spring 2008). *2.* Gwynedd Hat (*Knitscene* Fall 2010). *3.* Snowflake Jumper (*Knitscene* Fall 2008). *4.* Balsam Jacket (*Knitscene* Fall 2010). *5.* Insignia Shawl (*Knitscene* Summer 2011).

cecily glowik macdonald | **83**

In the name of simplicity, Cecily Glowik MacDonald designed this slouchy garter-stitch cap to focus on one cool technique—cinching the seaming yarn to gather the side seam. Try embellishing the hat with a brooch, ribbon, or decorative buttons. *designed by* **CECILY GLOWIK MACDONALD**

pinch hat

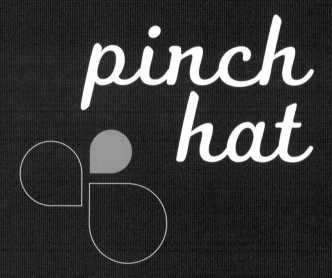

FINISHED SIZE
About 17¾" (45 cm) circumference and 9¼" (23.5 cm) tall.

YARN
Chunky weight (#5 Bulky).

SHOWN HERE Classic Elite Ariosa (90% merino, 10% cashmere; 87 yd [78 m]/50 g): #4857 ballard blue, 2 skeins.

NEEDLES
Size U.S. 9 (5.5 mm).

Adjust needle size if necessary to obtain the correct gauge.

NOTIONS
Removable marker; tapestry needle; one 2" (5 cm) decorative brooch.

GAUGE
14 sts and 30 rows (15 ridges) = 4" (10 cm) in garter st.

NOTES
● For ease of working, mark the right side of the work with a removable marker or piece of yarn looped through the front of a stitch.

HAT

CO 62 sts. Work in garter st (knit every row) until piece measures 7½" (19 cm) from CO, ending with a WS row.

Shape Crown

Row 1 (mark this side as RS) K2, k2tog, [k6, k2tog] 7 times, k2—54 sts rem.

Row 2 (WS) Knit.

Row 3 (RS) K2, k2tog, [k5, k2tog] 7 times, k1—46 sts rem.

Row 4 Knit.

Row 5 K2, k2tog, [k4, k2tog] 6 times, k6—39 sts rem.

Row 6 Knit.

Row 7 K2, k2tog, [k3, k2tog] 6 times, k5—32 sts rem.

Row 8 Knit.

Row 9 [K2, k2tog] 7 times, k4—25 sts rem.

Row 10 Knit.

Row 11 K1, [k1, k2tog] 7 times, k3—18 sts rem.

Row 12 Knit.

Row 13 [K2tog] 9 times—9 sts rem.

Cut yarn, leaving a 12" (30.5 cm) tail.

FINISHING

Thread tail on a tapestry needle, draw through rem sts, and pull tight to close top of hat. With same yarn and beg at top of hat, use mattress st for garter st (see Glossary) to sew seam down to CO edge. Pull yarn tight to gather cap along seam, then secure to WS.

Weave in loose ends. Pin brooch to hat near base of seam (or sew on decorative buttons or ribbon as desired).

For more information on **CECILY GLOWIK MACDONALD**, see profile on page 82.

Originally published in *Knitscene Easy 2010*

counting rows within a cable

by **KRISTIN ROACH**

WHILE KNITTING cables is simple, it's easy to lose track of which row you're on. The first step to creating picture-perfect cables is to learn the basics of row counting. The tip of your knitting needle is the best tool for this task. But first, you need to recognize a row of stitches in stockinette and reverse stockinette stitch.

THE KNIT SIDE (STOCKINETTE) Viewed from the right side, each stitch looks like a V *[1]*. You can count your rows by counting one V for each row and working your way from the top to the bottom. Always count the stitches on your needle as one row!

THE PURL SIDE (REVERSE STOCKINETTE) Viewed from the wrong side, each row is a paired line of dashes *[2]*. The dashes alternate slightly, so you can count one dash for each row and work straight up from the bottom to the top. Cables are often set on a ground of reverse stockinette stitch, with the cable worked in stockinette. Learning to count rows in this scenario is a good place to start.

Place the tip of your needle at the hole in your cable (where it twists). That is your cable row. From there you count rows up or down. Often the stitches of a cross row are extended slightly as they're stretched into their new position. In *[3]*, the medium gray row is the row where the cable twist (or cross) was worked. Count each V up from that point and include the stitches on your needle—here there are 5 rows after the cable row. You don't want to count the cross row itself here if you are trying to determine how many rows have been worked since the cross.

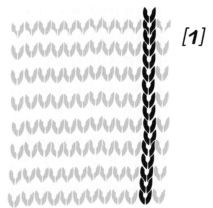

[1]

[2]

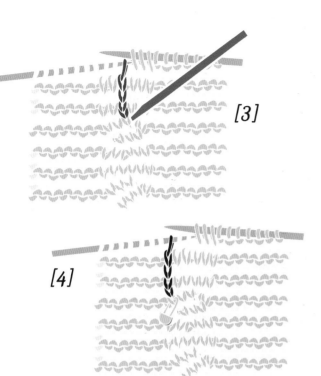

[3]

[4]

You can also place a stitch marker in the last stitch of the cable when you work your cable cross row. Count the Vs worked since the marked stitch to check which row you're on *[4]*. Just remember to place a new marker each time you work a cross row. If you're working multiple traveling cables, this is very helpful. Place a stitch marker in each cable.

If you're working embossed cables—cables worked in reverse stockinette—count rows in the same way but count purl dashes instead of knit Vs.

After learning to knit from her boyfriend, **KRISTIN ROACH** *started hanging around the LYS so much that they offered her a job. She now teaches fiber-art classes full time as well as hosts the local Sewing Rebellion. You can find current class schedules, free patterns, and links to all her online projects at http://krostudio.com/blog.*

quick cable tips

- Slip stitches purlwise to the cable needle to avoid twisting stitches.

- Metal cable needles can be handy for quick knits, but if you're using a slippery yarn, use a bamboo needle to avoid dropping stitches.

- If the difference between a left cross (3/3 LC) and a right cross (3/3 RC) eludes you, just remember: stitches held to the front = left cross, and stitches held to the back = right cross.

- Many types of cable needles are now available, and holding onto three needles can feel a little awkward at first. Finding the needle just right for you can make knitting cables much more enjoyable.

Shown at right are some of the typical cable needle shapes.

- Whichever cable needle you choose, use one that is smaller than your knitting needles to avoid stretching out the cable stitches.

- Cable needles in a pinch: A double-pointed needle is the best choice as a cable needle substitute, and some knitters swear by them for all their cable knitting needs. But looking around, you can produce some great alternatives—pencils, paper clips, scrap yarn, a little piece of wire, even a toothpick are all adequate cable needles when you need them to be.

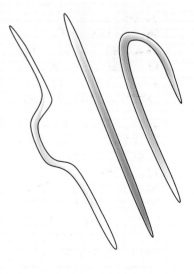

A plush mohair blend gives fuzzy depth to large cables and a roomy hood. Debbie O'Neill's most popular design, this hoodie makes for quick knitting and easy wearing with short sleeves, a chunky gauge, and no-fuss ribbed bands.

designed by **DEBBIE O'NEILL**

heather hoodie vest

FINISHED SIZE
About 35 (38, 41, 44, 47, 50)" (89 [96.5, 104, 112, 119.5, 127] cm) bust circumference, buttoned. Sweater shown measures 35" (89 cm).

YARN
Chunky weight (#5 Bulky).

SHOWN HERE Brown Sheep Lamb's Pride Bulky

(85% wool, 15% mohair; 125 yd [114 m]/113 g): #M-170 pine shadows, 7 (7, 8, 8, 9, 10) skeins.

NEEDLES
Size U.S. 10 (6 mm): 16" (40 cm) and 24" (60 cm) circular (cir).

Adjust needle size if necessary to obtain the correct gauge.

NOTIONS
Markers (m); cable needle (cn); stitch holders; tapestry needle; five 1" (2.5 cm) buttons.

GAUGE
14 sts and 22 rows = 4" (20 cm) in St st; 22-st cable panel measures 3¾" (9.5 cm) wide before blocking and 4¼" (11 cm) after blocking.

BACK

With longer cir needle, CO 73 (77, 83, 87, 93, 97) sts. Do not join.

Row 1 (WS) K0 (2, 0, 2, 0, 2), *p3, k2; rep from *, ending last rep k0 (2, 0, 2, 0, 2).

Row 2 (RS) P0 (2, 0, 2, 0, 2), *k3, p2; rep from *, ending last rep p0 (2, 0, 2, 0, 2).

Cont in rib as established until piece measures 2½" (6.5 cm) from CO, ending with a RS row.

Set-up row (WS) P6 (8, 11, 13, 16, 18), place marker (pm), k1, p2, k4, p3, M1P (see Glossary), p4, k4, p2, k1, pm, p19 (19, 19, 19, 19, 19), pm, k1, p2, k4, p3, M1P, p4, k4, p2, k1, pm, p6 (8, 11, 13, 16, 18)—75 (79, 85, 89, 95, 99) sts.

Next row (RS) Knit to m, sl m, work Row 2 of cable panel chart over 22 sts, sl m, knit to next m, sl m, work Row 2 of cable panel chart over 22 sts, sl m, knit to end.

Cont in patt, work Rows 3–18 of chart once, then rep Rows 1–18 until piece measures 21 (22, 23, 24, 25, 26)" (53.5 [56, 58.5, 61, 63.5, 66] cm) from CO, working sts outside m in St st and ending with a RS row.

Next row (WS) Work 24 (26, 28, 30, 32, 33) sts in patt, BO center 27 (27, 29, 29, 31, 33) sts for neck, work in patt to end—24 (26, 28, 30, 32, 33) sts rem for each shoulder.

Place sts on separate holders.

LEFT FRONT

With shorter cir needle, CO 33 (37, 40, 43, 47, 50) sts. Do not join.

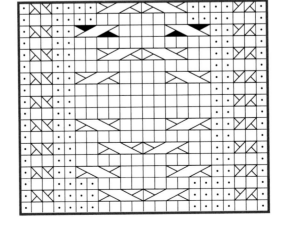

CABLE PANEL

☐ k on RS, p on WS

• p on RS, k on WS

⚊ slip 1 on cn, hold in BACK, k1, k1 from cn

⚊ slip 1 on cn, hold in FRONT, k1, k1 from cn

⚊ slip 3 on cn, hold in FRONT, k3, k3 from cn

⚊ slip 3 on cn, hold in FRONT, k3, k3 from cn

⚊ slip 3 on cn, hold in BACK, k3, p3 from cn

⚊ slip 3 on cn, hold in FRONT, p3, k3 from cn

☐ pattern repeat

Row 1 (WS) K0 (2, 0, 0, 2, 0), *p3, k2; rep from *, ending last rep k0 (2, 0, 0, 2, 0).

Row 2 (RS) P0 (2, 0, 0, 2, 0), *k3, p2; rep from *, ending last rep p0 (2, 0, 0, 2, 0).

Cont in rib as established until piece measures 2½" (6.5 cm) from CO, ending with a RS row.

Set-up row (WS) P6 (8, 8, 9, 10, 11), pm, k1, p2, k4, p3, M1P, p4, k4, p2, k1, pm, p6 (8, 11, 13, 16, 18)—34 (38, 41, 44, 48, 51) sts.

Next row (RS) Knit to m, sl m, work Row 2 of cable panel chart over 22 sts, sl m, knit to end.

Cont in patt, work Rows 3–18 of chart once, then rep Rows 1–18 until piece measures 17 (18, 19, 20, 21, 22)" (43 [45.5, 48.5, 51, 53.5, 56] cm) from CO, working sts outside m in St st and ending with a RS row.

Shape Neck

With WS facing, BO 4 (4, 4, 5, 5, 5) sts, work in patt to end—30 (34, 37, 39, 43, 46) sts rem.

Work 1 row even. At neck edge (beg of WS rows), BO 3 sts 1 (1, 1, 1, 2, 2) time(s), then BO 2 sts 1 (2, 2, 2, 2, 2) time(s), then dec 1 st every RS row 1 (1, 2, 2, 1, 3) time(s)—24 (26, 28, 30, 32, 33) sts rem. Work even in patt until piece measures same as back to shoulder, ending with a WS row. Place sts on holder.

RIGHT FRONT

With shorter cir needle, CO 33 (37, 40, 43, 47, 50) sts. Do not join.

Row 1 (WS) K0 (2, 0, 0, 2, 0), *p3, k2; rep from *, ending last rep k0 (2, 0, 0, 2, 0).

Row 2 (RS) P0 (2, 0, 0, 2, 0), *k3, p2; rep from *, ending last rep p0 (2, 0, 0, 2, 0).

Cont in rib as established until piece measures 2½" (6.5 cm) from CO, ending with a RS row.

Set-up row (WS) P6 (8, 11, 13, 16, 18), pm, k1, p2, k4, p3, M1P, p4, k4, p2, k1, pm, p6 (8, 8, 9, 10, 11)—34 (38, 41, 44, 48, 51) sts.

Next row (RS) Knit to m, sl m, work Row 2 of cable panel chart over 22 sts, sl m, knit to end.

Cont in patt, work Rows 3–18 of chart once, then rep Rows 1–18 of chart until piece measures 17 (18, 19, 20, 21, 22)" (43 [45.5, 48.5, 51, 53.5, 56] cm) from CO, working sts outside m in St st and ending with a WS row.

Shape Neck

With RS facing, BO 4 (4, 4, 5, 5, 5) sts, work in patt to end—30 (34, 37, 39, 43, 46) sts rem.

Work 1 row even. At neck edge (beg of RS rows), BO 3 sts 1 (1, 1, 1, 2, 2) time(s), then BO 2 sts 1 (2, 2, 2, 2, 2) time(s), then dec 1 st every RS row 1 (1, 2, 2, 1, 3) time(s)—24 (26, 28, 30, 32, 33) sts rem. Work even in patt until piece measures same as back to shoulder, ending with a WS row.

Place sts on holder.

FINISHING

Wet-block pieces to measurements. Weave in loose ends.

Seams

Using the three-needle method (see Glossary), BO shoulder sts tog. Measure 7½

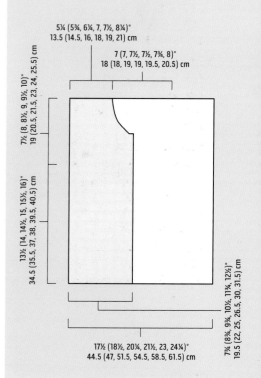

right front & back

5¼ (5¾, 6¼, 7, 7½, 8¼)"
13.5 (14.5, 16, 18, 19, 21) cm

7 (7, 7½, 7½, 7¾, 8)"
18 (18, 19, 19, 19.5, 20.5) cm

7½ (8, 8½, 9, 9½, 10)"
19 (20.5, 21.5, 23, 24, 25.5) cm

13½ (14, 14½, 15, 15½, 16)"
34.5 (35.5, 37, 38, 39.5, 40.5) cm

7¾ (8¾, 9¾, 10½, 11¾, 12½)"
19.5 (22, 25, 26.5, 30, 31.5) cm

17½ (18½, 20¼, 21½, 23, 24¼)"
44.5 (47, 51.5, 54.5, 58.5, 61.5) cm

Note *Schematic reflects wet-blocked measurements.*

(8, 8½, 9, 9½, 10)" (19 [20.5, 21.5, 23, 24, 25.5] cm) down from each shoulder seam and mark each side for base of armhole. With yarn threaded on a tapestry needle and beg at CO edge, sew side seams, stopping at marked base of armhole.

Armbands

With shorter cir needle and RS facing, pick up and knit 55 (60, 65, 70, 75, 80) sts evenly spaced around armhole opening. Pm and join for working in rnds. Work in k3, p2 rib for 2½" (6.5 cm). BO all sts in patt.

Hood

With longer cir needle, RS facing, and beg at right-front neck edge, pick up and knit 75 (75, 77, 77, 79, 81) sts evenly spaced around neck edge. Do not join. Work 3 rows in St st and *at the same time* pm each side of center st on last row—37 (37, 38, 38, 39, 40) sts each side of center st.

Inc row (RS) Knit to 1 st before first m, k1f&b (see Glossary), sl m, k1, sl m, k1f&b, knit to end—2 sts inc'd; 1 st each side of center st.

Work 7 rows even in St st. Rep inc row, then work 9 rows even in St st, ending with a WS row—2 sts inc'd. Rep inc row, then work 11 rows even in St st, ending with a WS row—2 sts inc'd. Rep inc row once more—83 (83, 85, 85, 87, 89) sts: 41 (41, 42, 42, 43, 44) sts each side of center st. Work even in St st until hood measures 12" (30.5 cm) from pick-up row.

Dec row (RS) Knit to 2 sts before first m, ssk, sl m, k1, sl m, k2tog, knit to end—2 sts dec'd.

Purl 1 row. Rep the last 2 rows 5 more times, then work dec row once more—69 (69, 71, 71, 73, 75) sts rem: 34 (34, 35, 35, 36, 37) sts each side of center st. Divide rem sts onto 2 needles, removing m and placing center st on second needle. With RS tog, use the three-needle method to BO sts tog.

Front Bands

With RS facing, mark placement of 5 buttonholes, one 1" (2.5 cm) above lower edge, one ½" (1.3 cm) below neck edge, and the others evenly spaced in between.

With longer cir needle, RS facing, and beg at lower right front edge, pick up and knit 248 (258, 268, 278, 288, 298) sts evenly spaced up right front, around hood, and down left front, ending at lower left front edge.

Next row (WS) P3, *k2, p3; rep from * to end.

Work 4 rows in rib as established, ending with a WS row.

Next row (buttonhole row) Work in rib as established and *at the same time* work a 2-st one-row buttonhole (see Glossary) at each m, adjusting markers as necessary to fall in the center of k3 ribs.

Work 5 more rows even in rib—11 rows total. BO all sts in patt.

Sew buttons to left front opposite buttonholes. Weave in loose ends. Block as desired.

DEBBIE O'NEILL is a computer engineer and prolific knit designer in Boulder, Colorado. Chosen as *Knitscene's* featured designer for the Winter/Spring 2011 issue, her designs focus on interesting stitch patterns and simple shapes that fit well. Her first book, *The Stitch Collection*, is available from Lark Books. She also publishes online at nuttycreations .wordpress.com.

Originally published in Fall 2009

Mathew Gnagy specializes in side-to-side knits and seamless construction—the Helleborus Yoke combines these methods to knitterly effect. The cabled yoke is worked from side to side in one long piece and shaped with short-rows to achieve the conical shape from underarm to neck. Plush textures, airy wool, and a rustic cool look have made this design popular; here Mathew gives us a new version in red with a collar slightly varied from the original. *designed by* **MATHEW GNAGY**

helleborus yoke

FINISHED SIZE
About 38 (43½, 52, 57½, 65½)" (96.5 [110.5, 132, 146, 166.5] cm) bust circumference, buttoned. Sweater shown measures 38" (96.5 cm).

YARN
Chunky weight (#5 Bulky).

SHOWN HERE Cascade Eco + (100% wool; 478 yd [437 m]/250 g): #8443 red, 2 (2, 3, 3, 4) skeins.

NEEDLES
BODY + SLEEVES size U.S. 10½ (6.5 mm): 24" (60 cm) circular (cir).

EDGING size U.S. 8 (5 mm): 24" (60 cm) cir.

Adjust needle size if necessary to obtain the correct gauge.

NOTIONS
Marker (m); removable markers; cable needle (cn); large stitch holder or spare cir needle; tapestry needle; seven ¾" (2 cm) buttons.

GAUGE
15 sts and 23 rows = 4" (10 cm) in moss st on larger needle; yoke cable panel = 7" (18 cm) wide.

NOTES
● Cardigan is worked from side to side in pieces and the pieces are joined to the yoke as they are worked.

● The yoke cable panel is worked continuously around the yoke.

stitch guide

MOSS STITCH (even number of sts)
Row 1 (RS) *K1, p1; rep from * to end.
Row 2 (WS) *K1, p1; rep from * to end.
Rows 3 and 4 *P1, k1; rep from * to end.
Rep Rows 1–4 for pattern.

MOSS STITCH (odd number of sts)
Row 1 (RS) *K1, p1; rep from * to last st, k1.
Row 2 (WS) *P1, k1; rep from * to last st, p1.
Row 3 *P1, k1; rep from * to last st, p1.
Row 4 *K1, p1; rep from * to last st, k1.
Rep Rows 1–4 for pattern.

RIGHT LIFTED INCREASE (RLI) Insert right
needle into side of st below st on left needle and
knit it, then work st on left needle—1 st inc'd.
RIGHT TWIST (RT) K2tog but do not drop sts
from left needle; knit first st again and drop
both sts from needle.
3/3RC Sl 3 sts onto cn and hold in back, k3, k3
from cn.
2/2RC Sl 2 sts onto cn and hold in back, k2, k2
from cn.
2/2LC Sl 2 sts onto cn and hold in front, k2, k2
from cn.

YOKE CABLE PANEL (worked over 32 sts)
Note Panel is shaped with short-rows (see
Glossary) on Rows 4, 6, 8, 16, 18, and 20.
Set-up row (WS) K2, p2, k2, p8, k2, p2, k2, p6,
k2, p2, k2.
Row 1 (RS; cable row) P2, RT (see above), p2,
3/3RC (see above), p2, RT, p2, 2/2RC (see
above), 2/2LC (see above), p2, RT, p2.
Rows 2, 12, and 14 (WS) Work sts as they
appear.
Row 3 P2, RT, p2, k6, p2, RT, p2, k8, p2, RT, p2.
Row 4 (WS) Work in patt to last 5 sts, wrap next
st, turn.

Row 5 (cable row) P1, 3/3RC, p2, RT, p2, 2/2LC,
2/2RC, p2, RT, p2.
Row 6 (WS) Work in patt to last 13 sts, wrap
next st, turn.
Row 7 P1, RT, p2, k8, p2, RT, p2.
Row 8 Work in patt to last 17 sts, wrap next st,
turn.
Row 9 (cable row) P1, 2/2RC, 2/2LC, p2, RT, p2.
Row 10 Work in patt to end, working wraps tog
with wrapped sts.
Row 11 P2, RT, p2, k6, p2, RT, p2, k8, p2, RT, p2.
Row 13 (cable row) P2, RT, p2, 3/3RC, p2, RT, p2,
2/2LC, 2/2RC, p2, RT, p2.
Row 15 P2, RT, p2, k6, p2, RT, p2, k8, p2, RT, p2.
Row 16 (WS) Work in patt to last 5 sts, wrap
next st, turn.
Row 17 (cable row) P1, 3/3RC, p2, RT, p2, 2/2RC,
2/2LC, p2, RT, p2.
Row 18 (WS) Work in patt to last 13 sts, wrap
next st, turn.
Row 19 P1, RT, p2, k8, p2, RT, p2.
Row 20 Work in patt to last 17 sts, wrap next
st, turn.
Row 21 (cable row) P1, 2/2LC, 2/2RC, p2, RT, p2.
Row 22 Work in patt to end, working wraps tog
with wrapped sts.

Row 23 P2, RT, p2, k6, p2, RT, p2, k8, p2, RT, p2.
Row 24 Work sts as they appear.
Rep Rows 1–24 for pattern.

SLEEVE CABLE PANEL (worked over 10 sts)
Note Cable rows may feel a bit awkward be-
cause cable is at edge of work.
Set-up row (WS) P2, k2, p6.
Row 1 (RS; cable row) 3/3RC, p2, RT.
Row 2 Work sts as they appear.
Row 3 K6, p2, RT.
Row 4 Rep Row 2.
Rep Rows 1–4 for pattern.

CENTER CABLE PANEL (worked over 32 sts)
Row 1 (RS) P2, RT, p2, 3/3RC, p2, RT, p2, 2/2RC,
2/2LC, p2, RT, p2.
Row 2 and all WS rows Work sts as they appear.
Row 3 P2, RT, p2, k6, p2, RT, p2, k8, p2, RT, p2.
Row 5 P2, RT, p2, 3/3RC, p2, RT, p2, 2/2LC,
2/2RC, p2, RT, p2.
Row 7 P2, RT, p2, k6, p2, RT, p2, k8, p2, RT, p2.
Row 8 Work sts as they appear.
Rep Rows 1–8 for pattern.

RIGHT FRONT

With larger needle, CO 70 (73, 76, 80, 83) sts. Do not join.

Set-up row (WS) Work Row 2 of moss st (see Stitch Guide) over 38 (41, 44, 48, 51) sts, place marker (pm), work set-up row of yoke cable panel (see Stitch Guide) over 32 sts.

Cont in patt, work Rows 1–24 of yoke cable panel 1 (1, 2, 2, 2) time(s), then work Rows 1–13 (1–21, 1–5, 1–13, 1–21) once more. *At the same time* inc 1 st on Row 15 (15, 13, 11, 11) of cable panel, then again every 14 (14, 12, 10, 10)th row 1 (2, 3, 4, 5) more time(s) as foll: (RS) Work yoke cable panel to m, sl m, RLI (see Stitch Guide), work in moss st to end—1 st inc'd. Work new sts into moss st; after all shaping and cable rows are complete, there will be 72 (76, 80, 85, 89) sts.

Shape Right Underarm

With WS facing, work in moss st to m, remove m, place next 32 sts on holder for yoke—40 (44, 48, 53, 57) sts rem. Work 8 (8, 12, 12, 16) rows in moss st. BO all sts loosely.

RIGHT SLEEVE

With larger needle, CO 12 (14, 16, 18, 20) sts. Do not join.

Set-up row (WS) Work 2 (4, 6, 8, 10) sts in rev St st (purl RS rows; knit WS rows), pm, work set-up row of sleeve cable panel (see Stitch Guide) over 10 sts.

Cont in patt, work Rows 1–4 of sleeve cable panel 2 (2, 3, 3, 4) times, then work Rows 1 and 2 once more.

Join Sleeve to Yoke

With WS of yoke facing and cont with sleeve needle and yarn, pm, work Row 14 (22, 6, 14, 22) of yoke cable panel across 32 held yoke sts—44 (46, 48, 50, 52) sts total.

Next row (RS) Work Row 15 (23, 7, 15, 23) of yoke cable panel to m, work Row 3 of sleeve cable panel to m, p2 (4, 6, 8, 10).

Next row K2 (4, 6, 8, 10), work Row 4 of sleeve cable panel to m, work Row 16 (24, 8, 16, 24) of yoke cable panel to end.

Work 41 (49, 57, 65, 73) more rows in patt, ending with RS Row 9 (1, 17, 9, 1) of yoke cable panel.

Finish Sleeve

With WS facing, work 12 (14, 16, 18, 20) sts in patt, place next 32 sts on holder for yoke. Cont in patt, work Rows 3 and 4 of sleeve cable panel once, then work Rows 1–4 of panel 2 (2, 3, 3, 4) times. Loosely BO all sts.

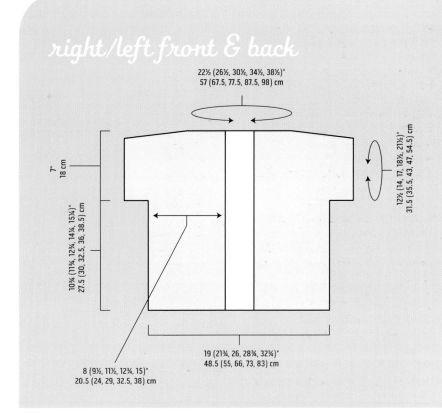

right/left front & back

22½ (26½, 30½, 34½, 38½)"
57 (67.5, 77.5, 87.5, 98) cm

7"
18 cm

12½ (14, 17, 18½, 21½)"
31.5 (35.5, 43, 47, 54.5) cm

10¾ (11¾, 12¾, 14¼, 15¾)"
27.5 (30, 32.5, 36, 38.5) cm

19 (21¾, 26, 28¾, 32¾)"
48.5 (55, 66, 73, 83) cm

8 (9½, 11½, 12¾, 15)"
20.5 (24, 29, 32.5, 38) cm

BACK

With larger needle, CO 40 (44, 48, 53, 57) sts. Do not join. Purl 1 WS row. Work 8 (8, 12, 12, 16) rows in moss st.

Join Back to Yoke

With WS of yoke facing and cont with back needle and yarn, pm, work Row 10 (2, 18, 10, 2) of yoke cable panel across 32 held yoke sts—72 (76, 80, 85, 89) sts total.

Next row (RS) Work Row 11 (3, 19, 11, 3) of yoke cable panel to m, work in moss st to end.

Cont in patt for 9 (7, 7, 7, 5) more rows, ending with Row 20 (10, 2, 18, 8) of panel.

Dec row (RS) Work next row of panel to m, dec 1 st (use k2tog or p2tog as needed to maintain moss st), work in moss st to end—1 st dec'd.

Cont in patt for 27 (37, 45, 53, 63) more rows, ending with Row 24 of panel and *at the same time* rep dec row every 12 (10, 10, 10, 10)th row 2 (3, 4, 5, 6) more times—69 (72, 75, 79, 82) sts rem.

Center Back

(RS) Work Row 1 of center cable panel (see Stitch Guide) to m, work in moss st to end.

Cont through Row 8 of panel. Place removable m at neck edge to denote center back neck. Cont in patt, work Rows 1–8 of center cable panel once more.

Resume working short-rows in yoke cable panel as foll:

Next row (RS) Work Row 1 of yoke cable panel to m, work in moss st to end.

Work 3 (7, 5, 3, 3) rows even in patt.

Inc row (RS) Work yoke cable panel to m, sl m, RLI, work in moss st to end—1 st inc'd.

Cont in patt for 32 (36, 46, 56, 64) more rows, ending with Row 13 (21, 5, 13, 21) of panel and *at the same time* rep inc row every 12 (10, 10, 10, 10)th row 2 (3, 4, 5, 6) more times, working new sts into moss st patt—72 (76, 80, 85, 89) sts.

Shape Left Underarm

With WS facing, work in moss st to m, remove m, place next 32 sts on holder for yoke—40 (44, 48, 53, 57) sts rem.

Work 8 (8, 12, 12, 16) rows in moss st. Loosely BO all sts.

LEFT SLEEVE

Work as for right sleeve.

LEFT FRONT

With larger needle, CO 40 (44, 48, 53, 57) sts. Do not join. Purl 1 WS row. Work 8 (8, 12, 12, 16) rows in moss st.

Join Left Front to Yoke

With WS of yoke facing and cont with left front needle and yarn, pm, work Row 10 (2, 18, 10, 2) of yoke cable panel across held yoke sts—72 (76, 80, 85, 89) sts total.

Next row (RS) Work Row 11 (3, 19, 11, 3) of yoke cable panel to m, work in moss st to end.

Work 7 (1, 3, 9, 7) more row(s) even in patt, ending with Row 18 (4, 22, 20, 10) of panel.

Dec row (RS) Work panel to m, dec 1 st (use k2tog or p2tog as needed to maintain moss st), work in moss st to end—1 st dec'd.

Cont in patt for 27 (41, 47, 49, 59) more rows, ending with Row 22 of panel and *at the same time* rep dec row every 14 (14, 12, 10, 10)th row 1 (2, 3, 4, 5) more time(s)—70 (73, 76, 80, 83) sts rem. BO all sts.

FINISHING
Sleeve Edging

With RS facing and smaller needle, pick up and knit 46 (50, 62, 66, 78) sts evenly spaced along lower edge of sleeve. Do not join. Work 12 rows in k2, p2 rib. With WS facing, BO all sts in patt.

With yarn threaded on a tapestry needle, sew sleeve and side seams.

Lower Edging

With RS facing and smaller needle, pick up and knit 34 (40, 48, 54, 64) sts evenly spaced along lower edge of left front, 76 (86, 104, 114, 130) sts along lower edge of back, and 34 (40, 48, 54, 64) sts along lower edge of right front—144 (166, 200, 222, 258) sts total. Do not join. Knit 12 rows. With WS facing, loosely BO all sts.

Collar

With smaller needle, CO 4 sts. Knit 8 rows.

Inc row (RS) K2, RLI, knit to end—1 st inc'd.

Knit 1 WS row. Rep the last 2 rows 7 more times—12 sts. Work short-rows (see Glossary) as foll:

SHORT-ROW SEQUENCE 1

Row 1 (RS) K2, RLI, knit to end—1 st inc'd.

Row 2 (WS) Knit to last 3 sts, wrap next st, turn.

Row 3 Knit.

Row 4 Knit to end, working wrap tog with wrapped st.

Rep the last 4 rows 2 (2, 7, 7, 12) more times—15 (15, 20, 20, 25) sts. Place removable m at beg of last row to denote end of shaping. Work even until longer edge of piece, slightly stretched, reaches from center front to center back m, ending with a WS row. Place removable m at beg of last row for center back neck. Work even until length from center back m matches length between center back m and m at end of shaping, ending with a WS row.

SHORT-ROW SEQUENCE 2

Row 1 (RS) K1, k2tog, knit to end—1 st dec'd.

Row 2 (WS) Knit to last 3 sts, wrap next st, turn.

Row 3 Knit.

Row 4 Knit to end, working wrap tog with wrapped st.

Rep last 4 rows 2 (2, 7, 7, 12) more times—12 sts rem.

Dec row (RS) K1, k2tog, knit to end—1 st dec'd.

Knit 1 row. Rep the last 2 rows 7 more times—4 sts rem. Knit 8 rows. BO all sts.

With yarn threaded on a tapestry needle, sew longer edge of collar to neckline, matching center markers.

Buttonband

With smaller needle, RS facing and beg at top of collar, pick up and knit 78 (82, 86, 90, 92) sts evenly spaced along left front, ending at bottom of lower edge. Knit 10 rows. With WS facing, BO all sts.

Buttonhole Band

With RS facing and smaller needle, pick up and knit 78 (82, 86, 90, 92) sts evenly spaced along right front edge. Knit 8 rows.

Buttonhole row (WS) K1 (3, 2, 1, 2), k2tog, yo, ssk, [k8 (8, 9, 10, 10), k2tog, yo, ssk] 6 times, k1 (3, 2, 1, 2).

Next row K2 (4, 3, 2, 3), [(k1, p1) in yo, k10 (10, 11, 12, 12)] 6 times, (k1, p1) in yo, k2 (4, 3, 2, 3).

Knit 2 rows. With WS facing, BO all sts.

Weave in loose ends. Block lightly with a steam iron over a damp cloth, taking care not to press too firmly—doing so will compromise the look of the cables.

Sew buttons to buttonband opposite buttonholes.

MATHEW GNAGY is author of *Knitting Off the Axis* (Interweave, 2011). His designs frequently feature cables and unusual constructions.

Originally published in Winter/Spring 2010

This sideways-knit shawlette is inlaid with a sweet leaf lace motif. Pointed edges and hand-painted silk laceweight yarn make for delicate appeal, while the knitting itself is not so intricate.

designed by **MANDY MOORE**

emily shawl

FINISHED SIZE
About 58" (147.5 cm) wide and 22½" (57 cm) deep at center point, after blocking.

YARN
Laceweight (#0 Lace).

SHOWN HERE Blue Moon Fiber Arts Geisha (70% kid mohair, 20% mulberry silk, 10% nylon; 995 yd [910 m]/227 g): jade, 1 skein (this should be enough for three shawls).

NEEDLES
Size U.S. 7 (4.5 mm): 24" (60 cm) or longer circular (cir).

Adjust needle size if necessary to obtain the correct gauge.

NOTIONS
Tapestry needle.

GAUGE
20 sts and 20 rows in lace patt = 4¼" (11 cm) wide and 3¼" (8.5 cm) long, after blocking.

NOTE
● Blocked gauge will vary throughout piece, as different parts of shawl will be stretched in different ways.

SHAWL

CO 3 sts. Purl 1 row. Work Rows 1–24 of Chart A—15 sts. Work Rows 1–20 of Chart B 3 times—45 sts. Work Rows 1–20 of Chart C 6 times—165 sts. Knit 1 RS row. Using the sewn method (see Glossary), BO all sts.

FINISHING

Weave in loose ends. Soak in warm water for 20 min. Squeeze out excess moisture and lay flat on a flat surface to block. Pin corners first, then pin points along shorter straight edges. Points along side edge are formed at the end of each column of yarnovers (end of Row 19 of Charts B and C); points along BO edge are formed at center of each pair of columns of yarnovers. There will be more points along BO edge than side edge. Once all points have been pinned, pin longer curved edge, placing 1 pin every 1–2" (2.5–5 cm). Note that curve may not be symmetrical. Allow to air-dry completely before removing pins.

CHART B

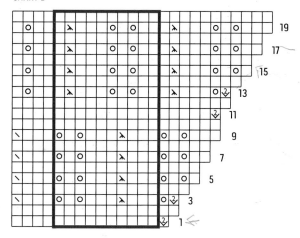

CHART C

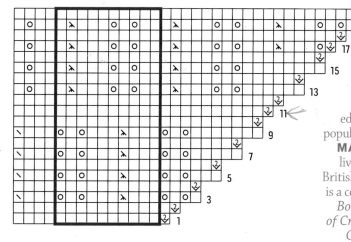

CHART A

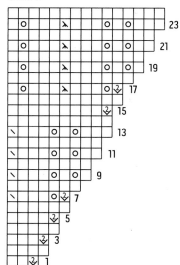

- ☐ k on RS, p on WS
- ◌ yo
- ╲ ssk
- ⋋ sl1, k2tog, psso
- ⤵ k1f&b on RS, p1f&b on WS
- ▢ pattern repeat

Senior technical editor of the uber-popular ezine *Knitty*, **MANDY MOORE** lives in Vancouver, British Columbia. She is a coauthor of *Yarn Bombing: The Art of Crochet and Knit Graffiti* (Arsenal Pulp Press, 2009) and blogs at yarnageddon.com.

Originally published in Winter/Spring 2010

reading lace charts

LACE KNITTING IS FUN because every row reveals a new effect—a dramatic new curve, hole, or slant. Lace lets you manipulate stitches in engaging ways, and it looks so darn pretty in the finished project! Some lace knitters prefer to work from row-by-row instructions, others prefer to work from charts. Following lace charts can be confusing to the beginner, but it's actually quite simple with some practice.

The Lace chart at right provides a good exercise. This eight-row, sixteen-stitch repeat involves yarnovers and decreases every other row. You can see that the symbols for yarnover (o) occur on even-numbered rows, which are the right-side rows. The odd-numbered rows are wrong-side rows and are worked without yarnovers.

When charts are worked in rows, you read right-side (RS) rows from right to left and you read wrong-side (WS) rows from left to right. In this chart, Row 1 is a WS row. To begin the chart, follow Row 1 from the left-hand side to the right-hand side, as follows: K2, p6, k2, p6. Easy enough?

Row 2 is a RS row and introduces our first yarnovers and decreases. In this lace pattern, the stitch count remains constant. This means that every yarnover (increase) is matched with a decrease so that the stitch count does not change. Work Row 2 as follows: K3, k2tog, k1, yo, p2, yo, k1, ssk, k3, p2.

The trickiest concept with lace charts is that the two stitches worked in a decrease are represented by a single symbol. When you work that k2tog, it results in one stitch but it required two stitches to begin with. Where did that second stitch box go?

The lace chart at right is used in the Lace Twist Mitts by Debbie O'Neill, *Knitscene* Fall 2009.

In this case, the yarnover replaces that "missing" stitch. Once you get to the first yarnover in Row 2, you've worked all the six stitches that precede the central p2. And with the decrease, you're actually left with only five stitches preceding the p2. But, you work a yarnover increase and, ta-da, you're back to six stitches. When you work Row 3, there will still be six stitches on that side of the central p2.

The fact is that the yarnover is stealing a stitch box in the chart. The stitch made by the yarnover did not exist in Row 1. But one stitch has been eliminated by the k2tog, so that box creates a convenient place to show the yarnover symbol.

Although this all sounds pretty technical, it's really very simple. Just knit the chart according to symbols as you see them. Work each stitch box as you come to it. You can think of a row in the chart as representing the stitches after the stitches had been knitted—for example, the k2tog results in one stitch (therefore one stitch box) and the yarnover creates one stitch (and therefore also occupies one stitch box).

NO STITCH? HUH?

Things get more complicated when the stitch count does not remain constant. The Double Fern Edging chart below shows what happens when yarnovers are not matched with the same number of decreases every row.

What are those gray boxes in the middle of the chart? These shaded boxes are "no stitch" symbols. They are inserted in a chart when a stitch has been decreased and therefore leaves a hole where there was a stitch previously. You can see on Row 2 that two stitches are decreased (with k2togs) without compensating yarnover increases. This effectively removes two stitches from the row, leaving you two fewer stitches to work individually on Row 2 and, subsequently, Row 3. By placing a no-stitch box next to each decrease, the chart-maker is telling you, "This stitch will no longer exist and should not be worked on this row." As discussed above, the k2tog is worked over two stitches but is represented by only one stitch box. Therefore, the second stitch box, removed by the decrease, becomes the black hole we call the no-stitch box. Just ignore the no-stitch box and do not work it. Work the stitch before the no-stitch box, then the stitch after the no-stitch box, and continue on your merry way.

If you work Row 2, you'll have two stitches fewer than you did when you finished Row 1. But on Row 3, there

are four yarnovers without matching decreases, leading to an increase of four stitches. You'll see the no-stitch boxes have disappeared and the right-hand end of the row has popped out to the right by two stitches. Two of the increases have replaced the missing stitches from Row 2, eradicating the no-stitch holes, and two of the increases have added to the breadth of the row, which is represented by the chart actually growing at the right edge.

Over the course of this chart, the stitch count changes several times, including a dramatic bind-off on Row 10, which is then compensated for with four increases on Row 1. If you work this pattern, the shape of the knitted fabric will undulate with the increased and decreased stitches, creating a decorative edging. The Lace chart from the first example does not change in stitch count and therefore makes a better allover or interior pattern for a project.

These basic principles apply to all lace charts, no matter how complex. Just remember: a yarnover is an increase, unless there's a compensating decrease somewhere in the same row. And a decrease is really a decrease unless there's a compensating yarnover somewhere in the same row. The corresponding yarnover and decrease don't have to be next to each other—or even close to each other—to work together. Have faith in the chart and knit it as you see it!

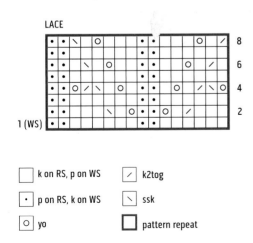

LACE

1 (WS)

DOUBLE FERN EDGING

	k on RS, p on WS		k2tog
	p on RS, k on WS		ssk
	yo		pattern repeat

	k on RS, p on WS		p2tog on RS; k2tog on WS
	p on RS, k on WS		bind off 1 st
	yo		no stitch
	k2tog on RS; p2tog on WS		pattern repeat

triangular shawls

by **MIRIAM FELTON**

THE TRIANGULAR SHAWL has been an iconic piece of women's clothing for hundreds of years, and it's still a favorite among knitters. Triangular shawls can be worn with the point hanging down the back, bunched up as a scarf under a coat, with the point in front and the ends tossed casually around the neck, or myriad other creative ways.

There are four basic ways to knit a triangle: top down, point up, wingspan down, and side to side.

TOP DOWN

Top-down construction begins in the middle of the wingspan edge. Each row is bisected by a center stitch. The rows get successively longer, and the bind-off is worked on the long bottom edges. The live stitches along the bottom edge create a unique canvas for knitted-on borders or crocheted edgings.

The shaping is usually accomplished by four increases worked every right-side row. One set of increases is placed just inside the edge stitches to form the wings, and one increase is placed on each side of a center stitch to form the central point. This shaping will result in a shawl with a wedge on each side of the center stitch; the stitch patterns will flow outward at two different angles toward the bind-off edge.

Upping the rate of increase at the edges will result in an upward curve in the wingspan, giving more of a crescent shape to the tail ends, while upping the rate of increase at the center stitch will result in a shawl shorter through the center back, with the wings angled up slightly.

POINT UP + WINGSPAN DOWN

Point-up construction begins at the bottom of the shawl at the base of the center point and increases up to the full width, while wingspan-down construction is exactly the opposite, beginning at the long upper edge and decreasing to the bottom point. Wingspan down is different from top down in that you cast on the number of stitches for the whole width of the top edge, unlike a top down for which you cast on just a few stitches and increase outward, with the selvedges becoming the wingspan.

For a longer point to both point up and wingspan down, you can increase or decrease two stitches on every other row, making the shawl about as long as it is wide. But if you change the rate of increase or decrease to two stitches every row instead of every other row, the triangle will become shorter and shallower, making it wider than it is long.

Both constructions can have center lines, but they are not essential as in top-down construction. Placing increases along the edge of the triangle only, and not in the center, presents a broad, uninterrupted canvas for a stitch pattern. For a directional stitch pattern, point-up construction would give you the correct stitch-pattern orientation, while wingspan-down would flip it 180 degrees. As new stitches are added or removed on the ends of every row, more pattern repeats can be inserted or removed.

Point-up construction can be used when you want to get the most from your yarn: You can bind off after completing any row and still be left with a finished triangle. If you did the same thing with a wingspan-down construction, you would be left with no bottom point on your shawl.

SIDE TO SIDE

Side-to-side construction begins at one side of the wingspan and is increased toward the center point, then decreased back down to the other side of the wingspan. In order to achieve the triangular shape, the increases and decreases must all be placed on one edge of the shawl instead of being evenly distributed across a row.

For a shallower triangle, one increase is worked every other row on one edge of the shawl to the center point and then one decrease every other row until the full wingspan is worked. For a deeper triangle (a longer point down the back) the rate of increase/decrease should be changed to one increase or decrease every row.

The shape results in an uninterrupted canvas for a stitch pattern, but one in which repeats can only be added and removed along the shaped edge. The stitch pattern would also be rotated 90 degrees from its original orientation.

FINAL CONSIDERATIONS

No matter which construction you use, the amount of stitch manipulation in the motifs within the shawl has a great impact on how severely the piece can be blocked. A stretchy stitch pattern will allow for more leeway in blocking than something such as a complicated cable, which makes the fabric contract. The increase used will also change the stretch factor of the shawl. For instance, a M1 increase is more restrictive than a yarnover.

One more thing to keep in mind is that blocking a triangular shawl has a huge impact on the shape. A standard top-down lace shawl can still be blocked to have a crescent curve in the wingspan if the edge stitches are stretchy enough. If you want a longer shawl, you can block it longer if you're willing to sacrifice some width.

Blocking a shawl (especially a lace shawl) is arguably the most important part of the process. Lace will often look like a tangled pile of string until it is soaked and pinned out. For a nonlace shawl, soaking may not be necessary, but pinning or smoothing out the finished piece will even out the stitches and pull everything into place. Pinning out the washed piece can be aided with wires or cotton string pulled taut to get a straight and even edge. Be sure to let the shawl dry completely before unpinning it.

MIRIAM FELTON's lace shawls and other designs have been published online and in print, and she also self-publishes patterns at www.mimknits.com. When she's not knitting, Miriam can be found frequenting Salt Lake City coffee shops while wearing her tiara.

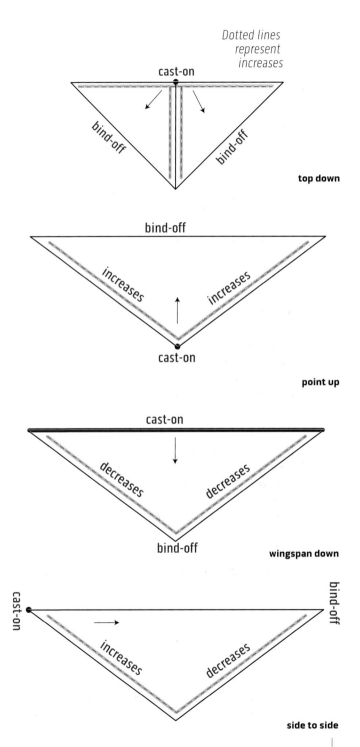

Dotted lines represent increases

cast-on

bind-off   bind-off

top down

bind-off

increases   increases

cast-on

point up

cast-on

decreases   decreases

bind-off

wingspan down

cast-on   bind-off

increases   decreases

side to side

A graphic mesh pattern makes a springy fabric that's perfect for a market bag. This sack is worked in the round, bottom up, from a flat base. When this pattern first came out, the trend in reusable shopping bags hadn't fully caught on—now this design should have mainstream appeal! *designed by* **CHRISSY GARDINER**

rutabaga bag

FINISHED SIZE
About 30¼" (77 cm) circumference and 13" (33 cm) tall, excluding strap.

YARN
DK weight (#3 Light).

SHOWN HERE Brown Sheep Cotton Fleece (80% cotton, 20% merino; 215 yd [197 m]/100 g): #CW-105 putty, 2 skeins.

NEEDLES
Size 10½ (6.5 mm): 24" (60 cm) circular (cir).

Adjust needle size if necessary to obtain the correct gauge.

NOTIONS
Stitch holder; marker (m); spare needle for three-needle bind-off; tapestry needle.

GAUGE
9 sts and 10 rows = 2" (5 cm) in mesh pattern.

stitch guide

CLUSTER Sl 2 sts with yarn in front (wyf), bring yarn between needles to back, wrapping it around sl sts, sl same 2 sts with yarn in back (wyb) onto left needle, bring yarn between needles to front, sl same 2 sts wyf onto right needle, bring yarn between needles to back—yarn is wrapped around 2 sl sts 1½ times.

MESH PATTERN (multiple of 4 sts)

Note Due to the nature of this patt, the beg of the rnd will move 1 st to the left every rnd.

Rnd 1 Remove marker (m), sl 1 with yarn in back (wyb), replace m, *k2tog, [yo] twice, ssk; rep from *.

Rnd 2 Remove m, sl 1 wyb, replace m, *k1, k1tbl, cluster (see Stitch Guide); rep from *.

Rep Rnds 1 and 2 for pattern.

BASE

CO 40 sts. Do not join; work back and forth in garter st (knit every row) for 30 rows to form a rectangle.

Pick-up rnd Turn the work 90 degrees, pick up and knit 14 sts evenly spaced along short side, 40 sts evenly spaced along CO edge, and 14 sts along other short side, ending at original beg of row—108 sts total.

Place marker (pm) to denote beg of rnd. Work garter st in the rnd (alternate purl 1 rnd, knit 1 rnd) for 6 rnds, ending with a knit rnd.

BODY

Inc rnd *[M1P (see Glossary), p4] 10 times, M1P, p3, [M1P, p4] 2 times, M1P, p3; rep from *—136 sts.

Work Rnds 1 and 2 of mesh patt (see Stitch Guide) 25 times, then work Rnd 1 once more—50 rows total in patt.

Next rnd Purl.

Dec Rnd 1 *K2, k2tog; rep from *—102 sts rem.

Purl 1 rnd, knit 1 rnd, purl 1 rnd.

Dec Rnd 2 K2tog, k2, *k2tog, k4; rep from * to last 2 sts, k2tog—84 sts rem.

Next rnd P12, BO 30 sts pwise, p12, BO 30 sts pwise—12 sts rem each side.

Place first set of 12 sts on a holder.

STRAP

Cont on 12 sts attached to working yarn, work strap in rows as foll:

Row 1 (RS) Sl 1 wyf, ssk, k6, k2tog, k1—10 sts rem.

Row 2 (WS) Sl 1 wyf, k9.

Row 3 Sl 1 wyf, ssk, k4, k2tog, k1—8 sts rem.

Row 4 Sl 1 wyf, k7.

Rep Row 4 until strap measures 19½" (49.5 cm), ending with a WS row. Cont as foll:

Row 1 (RS) Sl 1 wyf, k1f&b (see Glossary), k4, k1f&b, k1—10 sts.

Row 2 Sl 1 wyf, k9.

Row 3 Sl 1 wyf, k1f&b, k6, k1f&b, k1—12 sts.

Row 4 Sl 1 wyf, k11.

Move working sts to one tip of cir needle. Place sts from holder onto other tip of cir needle and hold the two tips parallel so sts of both strap ends are aligned with RS tog. With RS tog and spare needle, use the three-needle method (see Glossary) to graft sts tog.

FINISHING

Weave in loose ends. Block lightly.

CHRISSY GARDINER
lives in Portland, Oregon, in a house filled with kids, cats, rabbits, and yarn. She is author of the books *Toe-Up! Patterns and Worksheets to Whip Your Sock Knitting Into Shape* and *Indie Socks* (Sydwillow Press). You can find more at www .gardineryarnworks.com.

Originally published in Spring 2007

In her usual manner, Connie Chang Chinchio brings us understated design in an irresistible package. Shaped with waist darts, shoulder short-rows, and set-in sleeves, the silhouette of this hoodie is feminine, while the details are bold: deep cuffs, geometric neck placket, closely set buttons, and a rich marled yarn.

designed by **CONNIE CHANG CHINCHIO**

riding to avalon

FINISHED SIZE
About 34¾ (38¾, 42¾, 46½, 50¾)" (88.5 [98.5, 108.5, 118, 129] cm) bust circumference. Sweater shown measures 34¾" (88.5 cm).

YARN
DK weight (#3 Light).

SHOWN HERE Lorna's Laces Swirl DK (85% merino, 15% silk; 150 yd [138 m]/50 g): pewter, 8 (9, 10, 12, 13) skeins.

NEEDLES
Size U.S. 5 (3.75 mm): 24" to 36" (60 to 90 cm) circular (cir), depending on selected size.

Adjust needle size if necessary to obtain the correct gauge.

NOTIONS
Tapestry needle; stitch holders; markers (m) in 2 different colors; size F/5 (3.75 mm) crochet hook.

GAUGE
Gauge 22½ sts and 32 rows = 4" (10 cm) in St st, worked in rnds; 24 sts and 33 rows = 4" (10 cm) in purl twist st.

NOTES
◗ Sweater is worked in the round to underarms, then divided so that front and back are worked in rows to shoulders.

◗ As the body is knitted, darts are worked in the front and back (use same color markers

for all darts) and faux side seams are worked in garter stitch (use different color markers than for darts).

◗ Sleeves are worked in the round to underarm, then worked in rows for the cap shaping.

◗ When knitting in rows, the first and last stitches are worked in garter stitch (knit every row) for selvedges.

TWIST 2 PURL (TW2P) P2tog but leave both sts on left needle, purl the first st through the back loop (tbl), then drop both sts from left needle.

FAUX SIDE SEAM (worked over 1 st in garter st)

Rnd 1 Knit.

Rnd 2 Purl.

Rep Rnds 1 and 2 for pattern.

PURL TWIST STITCH (multiple of 4 sts)

Rows 1 and 3 (WS) Purl.

Row 2 (RS) *K2, Tw2p (see above); rep from *.

Row 4 *Tw2p, k2; rep from *.

Rep Rows 1–4 for pattern.

BODY

CO 200 (222, 244, 266, 290) sts. Join for working in rnds. Mark side seams and darts as foll (use one color marker for side seams and the other color marker for darts): Place marker (pm) for side seam (and beg of rnd), k25 (27, 30, 33, 36), pm for dart, k50 (57, 62, 67, 73), pm for dart, k25 (27, 30, 33, 36), pm for side seam, k25 (27, 30, 33, 36), pm for dart, k50 (57, 62, 67, 73), pm for dart, knit to end. Purl 1 rnd—1 garter ridge on RS.

Next rnd Set up faux side seams as foll: Sl first m, work 1 st in faux side seam patt (see Stitch Guide) knit to next seam m, sl m, work 1 st in faux side seam patt, knit to end.

Working faux side seam sts in garter st as established, cont in St st until piece measures 3 (3, 3¼, 3½, 4)" (7.5 [7.5, 8.5, 9, 10] cm) from CO.

Shape Waist

Dec rnd *Work in patt to dart m, sl m, ssk, work to 2 sts before next dart m, k2tog; rep from * once, work to end—4 sts dec'd.

Rep dec rnd every 8th rnd 4 more times—180 (202, 224, 246, 270) sts rem. Work 13 rnds even.

Inc rnd *Work in patt to dart m, sl m, M1 (see Glossary), work to next dart m, M1, sl m; rep from * once, work to end—4 sts inc'd.

Rep inc rnd every 10th rnd 3 more times—196 (218, 240, 262, 286) sts. Remove dart m and work even until piece measures 14½ (14½, 14¾, 15, 15½)" (37 [37, 37.5, 38, 39.5] cm) from CO.

Divide for Armholes

With RS facing, k2tog (eliminating faux seam st), BO 5 (6, 8, 8, 8) sts, knit to next seam m, sl m, k1, turn, place rem 97 (108, 119, 130, 142) sts on holder to work later for front.

BACK

Work back sts back and forth in rows as foll:

With WS facing, p2tog (eliminating faux seam st), BO 5 (6, 8, 8, 8) sts, purl to end—87 (96, 103, 114, 126) sts rem.

BO 0 (0, 0, 3, 6) sts at beg of next 0 (0, 0, 2, 2) rows—87 (96, 103, 108, 114) sts rem. Dec 1 st each end of needle every RS row 6 (7, 8, 8, 8) times—75 (82, 87,

92, 98) sts rem. Work even in St st until armholes measure 7½ (8, 8½, 8¾, 9¼)" (19 [20.5, 21.5, 22, 23.5] cm), ending with a WS row.

Shape Neck + Left Shoulder

Work short-rows (see Glossary) as foll:

With RS facing, k20 (23, 25, 26, 29) for right shoulder, BO 35 (36, 37, 40, 40) sts for neck, knit to last 10 (11, 12, 13, 14) sts, wrap next st, turn, purl to end.

Next row (RS) Knit, working wrap tog with wrapped st.

Place rem 20 (23, 25, 26, 29) sts on holder for left shoulder.

Shape Right Shoulder

With WS facing, join yarn to neck edge. Purl to last 10 (11, 12, 13, 14) sts, wrap next st, turn, knit to end.

Next row (WS) Purl, working wrap tog with wrapped st.

Place rem 20 (23, 25, 26, 29) sts on holder for right shoulder.

FRONT

With RS facing, join yarn to side edge of held front sts. Mark center 9 (10, 9, 10, 10) sts.

Next row (RS) BO 5 (6, 8, 8, 8) sts, knit to marked center sts, BO 9 (10, 9, 10, 10) center sts for neck, knit to end.

Next row (WS) BO 5 (6, 8, 8, 8) sts, purl to neck edge; join yarn to opposite neck edge (to work both sides at the same time), purl to end—39 (43, 47, 52, 58) sts rem each side.

Cont to shape armholes as for back and *at the same time* dec 1 st at each neck edge every 5th row once, then every 6th row

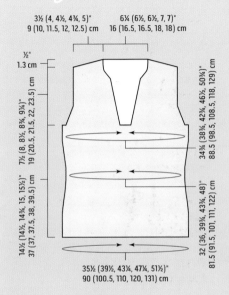

body

3½ (4, 4½, 4¾, 5)"
9 (10, 11.5, 12, 12.5) cm

6¼ (6½, 6½, 7, 7)"
16 (16.5, 16.5, 18, 18) cm

½"
1.3 cm

7½ (8, 8½, 8¾, 9¼)"
19 (20.5, 21.5, 22, 23.5) cm

34¾ (38¾, 42¾, 46¾, 50¾)"
88.5 (98.5, 108.5, 118, 129) cm

14½ (14½, 14¾, 15, 15½)"
37 (37, 37.5, 38, 39.5) cm

32 (36, 39¾, 43¾, 48)"
81.5 (91.5, 101, 111, 122) cm

35½ (39½, 43¾, 47¾, 51½)"
90 (100.5, 110, 120, 131) cm

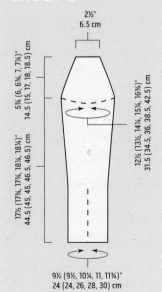

sleeve

2½"
6.5 cm

5¾ (6, 6¾, 7, 7¼)"
14.5 (15, 17, 18, 18.5) cm

12½ (13¾, 14¾, 15¼, 16¾)"
31.5 (34.5, 36, 38.5, 42.5) cm

17½ (17¾, 17¾, 18¼, 18¼)"
44.5 (45, 45, 46.5, 46.5) cm

9½ (9½, 10¼, 11, 11¾)"
24 (24, 26, 28, 30) cm

7 more times—25 (28, 31, 33, 36) sts rem each side. Work even until armholes measure 6¼ (6½, 7, 7¼, 7¾)" (16 [16.5, 18, 18.5, 19.5] cm), ending with a WS row.

Shape Neck

BO 3 (3, 4, 5, 5) sts at each neck edge once, then dec 1 st at each neck edge every RS row 2 times—20 (23, 25, 26, 29) sts rem each side. Cont even until armholes measure 7½ (8, 8½, 8¾, 9¼)" (19 [20.5, 21.5, 22, 23.5] cm).

Shape Shoulders

Work shoulder shaping as for back.

SLEEVES

CO 58 (58, 62, 66, 70) sts. Do not join.

Next row (WS) K1 (selvedge st), work purl twist st (see Stitch Guide) to last st, k1 (selvedge st).

Knitting the first and last st of every row, cont as established until piece measures 6½ (6½, 6½, 7, 7)" (16.5 [16.5, 16.5, 18, 18] cm) from CO, ending with a RS row.

Dec row: (WS) Purl and *at the same time* dec 5 (4, 4, 4, 4) sts evenly spaced—53 (54, 58, 62, 66) sts rem.

Pm and join for working in rnds.

Next rnd: K26 (27, 29, 31, 33), pm for center of sleeve, knit to end.

Knit 5 rnds even.

Inc rnd: Work to center-of-sleeve m, M1, sl m, k1, M1, work to end—2 sts inc'd.

Rep inc rnd every 10 (8, 8, 7, 6)th rnd 8 (10, 10, 11, 13) times—71 (76, 80, 86, 94) sts. Work even until piece measures 17½ (17¾, 17¾, 18¼, 18¼)" (44.5 [45, 45, 46.5, 46.5] cm) from CO.

Shape Cap

Work back and forth in rows as foll:

Next row (RS) BO 5 (6, 8, 8, 8) sts, knit until 66 (70, 72, 78, 86) sts have been worked, turn.

Next row (WS) BO 5 (6, 8, 8, 8) sts, purl to end—61 (64, 64, 70, 78) sts rem.

BO 0 (0, 0, 3, 6) sts at beg of next 0 (0, 0, 2, 2) rows—61 (64, 64, 64, 66) sts rem. Dec 1 st each end of needle every row 3 (3, 0, 0, 0) times, then every other row 5 (6, 8, 8, 8) times, then every 4th row 4 (4, 4, 5, 5) times, then every other row 5 (6, 6, 6, 7) times—27 (26, 26, 26, 26) sts rem. BO 3 sts at beg of next 4 rows—15 (14, 14, 14, 14) sts rem. BO all sts.

FINISHING

Block pieces to measurements.

Left Front Band

With RS facing and beg at neck edge, pick up and knit 40 (43, 46, 48, 51) sts evenly spaced along shaped edge of left front, ending at center front BO sts.

Next row (WS) Work in purl twist st.

Inc row (RS) Work purl twist st to last st, M1, k1—1 st inc'd.

Rep inc row every RS row 3 more times—44 (47, 50, 52, 55) sts. Work even until band measures 1½ (1¾, 1½, 1¾, 1¾)" (3.8 [4.5, 3.8, 4.5, 4.5] cm) from pick-up row, ending with a RS row. BO all sts.

Right Front Band

With RS facing and beg at center front BO sts, pick up and knit 40 (43, 46, 48, 51) sts evenly spaced along shaped edge of right front, ending at neck edge.

Next row (WS) Work in purl twist st.

Inc row (RS) K1, M1, work purl twist st to end—1 st inc'd.

Rep inc row every RS row 3 more times—44 (47, 50, 52, 55) sts. Work even until band measures 1½ (1¾, 1½, 1¾, 1¾)" (3.8 [4.5, 3.8, 4.5, 4.5] cm) from pick-up row, ending with a RS row.

Work button flap as foll:

BO row (WS) BO 18 (19, 21, 22, 23) sts, dec 1 st, work to end—25 (27, 28, 29, 31) sts rem.

Dec row (RS) Dec 1 st, work to end—1 st dec'd.

Rep dec row every 4th row and *at the same time* dec 1 st at beg of every WS row until 5 sts rem. BO as foll: K2tog, k1, pass 2nd st over first st; k2tog, pass 2nd st over first st; rep from * until all sts are BO.

Hood

With RS facing and beg at center front edge of right front band, pick up and knit 91 (95, 95, 101, 101) sts evenly spaced around neck shaping, ending at center front edge of left band.

Next row (WS) K1, p45 (47, 47, 50, 50), pm, purl to 1 st before end, k1.

Working in purl twist st, work even for 8 rows.

Inc row (RS) Work to m, M1, sl m, k1, M1, work to end—2 sts inc'd.

Rep inc row every 10th row 5 more times—103 (107, 107, 113, 113) sts. Work even until hood measures 12¾" (32.5 cm) from pick-up row, ending with a WS row.

Shape Top

With RS facing and keeping in patt as established, work 51 (53, 53, 56, 56) sts, BO 1 st, work to end. Work short-rows to shape top of hood as foll:

Left Side

Next row With WS facing, work to last 8 (8, 8, 9, 9) sts, wrap next st, turn, work in patt to end.

Next row Work to last 16 (16, 16, 18, 18) sts, wrap next st, turn, work to end.

Next row Work to last 24 (24, 24, 27, 27) sts, wrap next st, turn, work to end.

Next row Work to last 32 (32, 32, 36, 36) sts, wrap next st, turn, work to end.

Next row Work to last 40 (40, 40, 45, 45) sts, wrap next st, turn, work to end.

Next row Work all sts, working wraps tog with wrapped sts.

Place 51 (53, 53, 56, 56) sts on holder.

Right Side

With WS facing, join yarn at BO center st. Work short-rows as for left side, reversing shaping.

Seams

Use the three-needle method (see Glossary) to BO shoulder sts tog. With yarn threaded on a tapestry needle, sew sleeve caps into armholes. Sew bottom edge of left-front band to the BO center sts at center-front opening. Sew bottom edge of right-front band to the BO center sts, lapping right band over left. Using the three-needle method, BO the rem hood sts tog.

Button Loops (make 16)

With crochet hook and leaving a 6" (15 cm) tail, make a chain (see Glossary for crochet instructions) about 2" (5 cm) long. Work a sc into each ch and join into a ring. Break yarn, leaving a 6" (15 cm) tail.

Use tails to attach 6 loops evenly spaced along the outer edge of each split cuff.

Attach rem 4 loops evenly spaced along asymmetrical flap of right front band.

Sew buttons opposite button loops. Weave in loose ends.

Armed with a PhD in physics, a background in environmental science, and a growing portfolio of knitwear designs, **CONNIE CHANG CHINCHIO** combines practicality and a love of pretty things. Her first book, *Knitted Textures*, will be available from Interweave in 2012.
Originally published in Fall 2008

Two to three skeins are all you need for this super-cute pullover. A basic T shape is worked in two pieces—front and back—and topped with a deep cowl neck. Melissa Wehrle designed the sweater as one of four looks for her exclusive *Knitscene* collection, which was incredibly popular upon release of the Fall 2009 issue.

designed by **MELISSA WEHRLE**

berkshire dolman sweater

FINISHED SIZE
About 30 (33, 36, 40½, 45)" (76 [84, 91.5, 103, 114.5] cm) bust circumference. Sweater shown measures 33" (84 cm).

YARN
Chunky weight (#5 Bulky).

SHOWN HERE Cascade Ecological Wool (100% wool; 478 yd [523 m]/250 g): #8019 medium heather gray, 2 (2, 3, 3, 3) skeins.

NEEDLES
BODY + SLEEVES size U.S. 10 (6 mm).

EDGING size U.S. 9 (5.5 mm): 20" (50 cm) circular (cir) and set of 5 double-pointed (dpn).

Adjust needle size if necessary to obtain the correct gauge.

NOTIONS
Markers (m); stitch holder; tapestry needle; four ⅞" (2.2 cm) buttons; sharp-point sewing needle and matching thread.

GAUGE
15 sts and 22 rows = 4" (10 cm) in St st on larger needles; 21 sts and 24 rows = 4" (10 cm) in k2, p2 rib on smaller needles, unstretched.

BACK

With smaller cir needle, CO 58 (62, 70, 78, 86) sts. Do not join.

Next row (WS) *P2, k2; rep from * to last 2 sts, p2.

Cont in rib as established until piece measures 4" (10 cm) from CO.

Change to larger needles and St st.

Shape Waist

Dec row (RS) K1, ssk, knit to last 3 sts, k2tog, k1—2 sts dec'd.

Rep dec row every 4 (6, 4, 4, 4) rows 1 (2, 4, 4, 2) time(s), then every 6 (8, 0, 0, 6) rows 2 (1, 0, 0, 2) time(s)—50 (54, 60, 68, 76) sts rem. Work 5 rows even.

Inc row (RS) K1, M1 (see Glossary), knit to last st, M1, k1—2 sts inc'd.

Rep inc row every 8 (6, 8, 8, 8) rows 2 (3, 3, 3, 3) more times—56 (62, 68, 76, 84) sts. Work even until piece measures 11¾ (12, 12¼, 12¼, 12¾)" (30 [30.5, 31, 31, 32.5] cm) from CO, ending with a WS row.

Shape Sleeves

Working 1 st in from each edge, inc 1 st each end of needle every row 3 times, then every RS row 2 times as foll: (RS) K1, M1, knit to last st, M1, k1; (WS) P1, M1P (see Glossary), purl to last st, M1P, p1. There will be 66 (72, 78, 86, 94) sts after all shaping is complete.

Next row (WS) Work to end, then use the backward-loop method (see Glossary) to CO 32 (33, 33, 34, 34) sts—98 (105, 111, 120, 128) sts.

Next row (RS) Work to end, then use the backward-loop method to CO 32 (33, 33, 34, 34) more sts—130 (138, 144, 154, 162) sts.

Work even in St st until lower edge of sleeve measures 6¼ (6½, 6¾, 7¼, 7¾)" (16 [16.5, 17, 18.5, 19.5] cm) from last CO, ending with a WS row.

Shape Shoulders

BO 8 (8, 9, 10, 10) sts at beg of next 6 rows—82 (90, 90, 94, 102) sts rem.

Next row (RS) BO 8 (8, 9, 10, 10) sts, work until there are 16 (19, 18, 18, 22) sts on right needle, turn work, place rem sts on holder to work later for left back and neck.

Work right back sts back and forth in rows as foll:

Next row (WS) P2tog, purl to end—1 st dec'd.

Next row (RS) BO 8 (8, 9, 10, 10) sts, knit to last 2 sts, k2tog—6 (9, 7, 6, 10) sts rem.

Next row P2tog, purl to end—1 st dec'd.

Next row (RS) BO rem 5 (8, 6, 5, 9) sts.

With RS facing, rejoin yarn at neck edge and BO center 34 (36, 36, 38, 38) sts for back neck, work across rem 24 (27, 27, 28, 32) sts.

Next row (WS) BO 8 (8, 9, 10, 10) sts, work to last 2 sts at neck edge, ssp (see Glossary).

Next row (RS) Ssk, work to end.

Next row (WS) BO 8 (8, 9, 10, 10) sts, work to last 2 sts, ssp.

Work 1 row even. BO rem 5 (8, 6, 5, 9) sts.

FRONT

CO and work as for back until piece measures 19 (19½, 19¾, 20¼, 21)" (48.5 [49.5, 50, 51.5, 53.5] cm) from CO, ending with a WS row—130 (138, 144, 154, 162) sts rem.

Next row (RS) Work 57 (60, 63, 68, 72) sts, place next 73 (78, 81, 86, 90) sts on holder for right front and neck.

Shape Left Front Neck + Shoulder

Next row (WS) BO 4 sts, work to end.

Dec 1 st at neck edge every row 8 (8, 8, 9, 9) times and *at the same time* when lower edge of sleeve measures 6¼ (6½, 6¾, 7¼, 7¾)" (16 [16.5, 17, 18.5, 19.5] cm) from last CO, shape shoulder as foll:

BO 8 (8, 9, 10, 10) sts at beg of next 5 RS rows—5 (8, 6, 5, 9) sts rem. Work 1 row even. BO all sts.

Shape Right Front Neck + Shoulder

With RS facing, rejoin yarn at neck edge and BO center 16 (18, 18, 18, 18) sts—57 (60, 63, 68, 72) sts rem for right front.

Cont on right-front sts only, BO 4 more sts at neck edge, work to end—53 (56, 59, 64, 68 sts rem. Dec 1 st at neck edge every row 8 (8, 8, 9, 9) times and *at the same time* when lower edge of sleeve measures 6¼ (6½, 6¾, 7¼, 7¾)" (16 [16.5, 17, 18.5, 19.5] cm) from last CO, shape shoulder as foll:

BO 8 (8, 9, 10, 10) sts at beg of next 5 WS rows—5 (8, 6, 5, 9) sts rem. Work 1 row even. BO all sts.

FINISHING

Block pieces to measurements. With yarn threaded on a tapestry needle, sew shoulder seams. Sew sleeve and side seams.

Cowl

With smaller cir needle, CO 88 (96, 96, 100, 100) sts. Place marker (pm) and join for working in rnds. Work in k2, p2 rib until piece measures 9 (9½, 9½, 10, 10)"

(23 [24, 24, 25.5, 25.5] cm) from CO. BO all sts in patt. Sew tube to neck edge of sweater.

Cuffs

With smaller dpn, RS facing, and beg at underarm seam, pick up and knit 40 (40, 48, 48, 56) sts evenly spaced around lower edge of sleeve. Pm and join for working in rnds. Work in k2, p2 rib until rib measures 5½" (14 cm) from pick-up rnd. Loosely BO all sts in patt. Fold up cuff. With sewing needle and thread, sew 2 buttons evenly spaced on outside of each cuff to hold cuff in place.

Weave in loose ends.

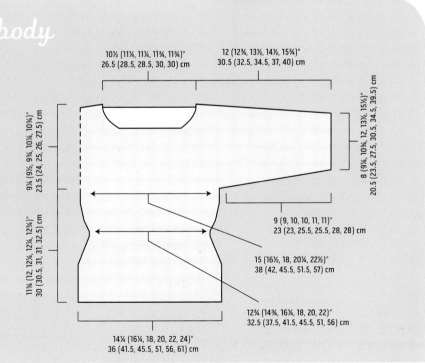

body

10½ (11¼, 11¼, 11¾, 11¾)"
26.5 (28.5, 28.5, 30, 30) cm

12 (12¾, 13½, 14½, 15¾)"
30.5 (32.5, 34.5, 37, 40) cm

9¼ (9½, 9¾, 10¼, 10¾)"
23.5 (24, 25, 26, 27.5) cm

8 (9¼, 10¾, 12, 13½, 15½)"
20.5 (23.5, 27.5, 30.5, 34.5, 39.5) cm

11¾ (12, 12¼, 12¼, 12¾)"
30 (30.5, 31, 31, 32.5) cm

9 (9, 10, 10, 11, 11)"
23 (23, 25.5, 25.5, 28, 28) cm

15 (16½, 18, 20¼, 22½)"
38 (42, 45.5, 51.5, 57) cm

12¾ (14¾, 16¼, 18, 20, 22)"
32.5 (37.5, 41.5, 45.5, 51, 56) cm

14¼ (16¼, 18, 20, 22, 24)"
36 (41.5, 45.5, 51, 56, 61) cm

By trade, **MELISSA WEHRLE** is a knitwear designer for the fashion industry. She combines this with a second career—designing handknits—in New York City. Melissa was chosen as the featured designer for the Fall 2009 issue and has been a regular contributor to the magazine. You can see more of her work at neoknits.com

Originally published in Fall 2009

Spokelike ribs are the only decoration in Carol Sulcoski's little hat. This design demonstrates what *Knitscene* is all about—simple knitting and cool design. A switch from k4, p1 to p4, k1 rib creates visual interest and a snug fit.

designed by **CAROL SULCOSKI**

ribby toque

FINISHED SIZE
About 19" (48.5 cm) circumference, unstretched.

YARN
Worsted weight (#4 Medium).

SHOWN HERE Filatura di Crosa Zara Plus (100% superwash merino; 77 yd [70 m]/50 g): #439 olive green, 2 skeins.

NEEDLES
Size U.S. 8 (5 mm): 16" (40 cm) circular (cir) and set of 4 double-pointed (dpn).

Adjust needle size if necessary to obtain the correct gauge.

NOTIONS
Markers (m); tapestry needle.

GAUGE
20 sts and 24 rnds = 4" (10 cm) in k4, p1 rib, worked in rnds and slightly stretched.

K4, P1 RIB (multiple of 5 sts)
All rnds *K4, p1; rep from *.

P4, K1 RIB (multiple of 5 sts)
All rnds *P4, k1; rep from *.

HAT

With cir needle, CO 100 sts. Place marker (pm) and join for working in rnds. Work in k4, p1 rib (see Stitch Guide) until piece measures 2¼" (5.5 cm) from CO. Change to p4, k1 rib (see Stitch Guide) and work even until piece measures 5½" (14 cm) from CO.

Shape Crown

Note Change to dpn when there are too few sts to fit comfortably on cir needle.

Rnd 1 *P1, p2tog, p1, k1; rep from * —80 sts rem.

Rnd 2 *P3, k1; rep from *.

Rnd 3 *P2tog, p1, k1; rep from * —60 sts rem.

Rnd 4 *P2, k1; rep from *.

Rnd 5 *P2tog, k1; rep from * —40 sts rem.

Rnd 6 *P1, k1; rep from *.

Rnd 7 *K2tog; rep from *—20 sts rem.

Rnd 8 *K2tog; rep from *—10 sts rem.

Break yarn, leaving a 10" (25.5 cm) tail.

FINISHING

Thread tail on a tapestry needle, draw through rem sts, pull tight to close hole, and fasten off on WS. Weave in loose ends.

CAROL SULCOSKI is owner of Black Bunny Fibers, creators of hand-dyed yarns and spinning fiber. She is author of *Knitting Socks with Handpainted Yarn* (Interweave, 2008), co-author of *Knit So Fine* (Interweave, 2008), and she blogs at goknitinyourhat .blogspot.com.

Originally published in Winter/Spring 2010

Overt girliness takes on a kind of toughness in this formfitting corset top. Drastic increases and decreases create ruched bands at bodice and strap, while a low wide neck and allover rib suggest a Moulin Rouge silhouette. Go for negative ease and light layering.

designed by **MICHELE ROSE ORNE**

molly ringwald

FINISHED SIZE
About 34½ (37½, 40, 43, 46)" (87.5 [95, 101.5, 109, 117] cm) bust circumference. Top shown measures 34" (86.5 cm).

YARN
DK weight (#3 Light).

SHOWN HERE Classic Elite Classic Silk (50% cotton, 30% silk, 20% nylon; 135 yd (124 m)/50 g): #6919 primrose, 5 (6, 6, 7, 7) balls.

NEEDLES
Size U.S. 6 (4 mm).

Adjust needle size if necessary to obtain the correct gauge.

NOTIONS
Markers (m); tapestry needle; size B/1 (2.25 mm) crochet hook.

GAUGE
22 sts and 28 rows = 4" (10 cm) in k3, p1 rib.

NOTES
● The front and back are worked separately; the straps are worked as part of the front, then joined to the back.

● The ruffled cap sleeves are worked from stitches picked up along armhole edges of the straps.

FRONT

CO 95 (103, 111, 119, 127) sts.

Row 1 (WS) P1, *k1, p3; rep from * to last 2 sts, k1, p1.

Row 2 (RS) K1, *p1, k3; rep from * to last 2 sts, p1, k1.

Rows 3–7 Rep Rows 1 and 2 two more times, then rep Row 1 once more.

Pointelle row (RS) K1, *p1, k1, yo, ssk; rep from * to last 2 sts, p1, k1.

Work 1 WS row in rib patt.

Dec row (RS) K1, ssk, work in patt to last 3 sts, k2tog, k1—2 sts dec'd.

Work 7 rows even in rib. Rep the last 8 rows 3 more times, then rep dec row once more—85 (93, 101, 109, 117) sts rem. Work 16 rows even in rib.

Note Increases, yoke patt, and armhole shaping are worked simultaneously; read all the way through the foll sections before proceeding.

Inc row (RS) K1, M1 (see Glossary), work in patt to last st, M1, k1—2 sts inc'd.

Work 7 rows even in rib. Rep the last 8 rows 3 more times, then rep inc row once—95 (103, 111, 119, 127) sts.

At the same time when piece measures 12½ (12½, 13, 13, 13½)" (31.5 [31.5, 33, 33, 34.5] cm) from CO, place marker (pm) each side of center 51 sts on last WS row and work yoke patt as foll:

Row 1 (RS) Work in established rib to m, p51, work in established rib to end.

Row 2 (WS) Work in rib to m, p51, work in rib to end.

Rows 3 and 4 Rep Rows 1 and 2.

Row 5 (RS) Work in rib to m, *k1, M1; rep from * to 1 st before m, k1, work in rib to end—145 (153, 161, 169, 177) sts.

Rows 6–9 Work in rib to m, work center 101 sts in St st (purl WS rows; knit RS rows), work in rib to end.

Row 10 (WS) Work in rib to m, *p2tog; rep from * to 1 st before m, p1, work in rib to end—95 (103, 111, 119, 127) sts rem.

Rep Rows 1–10 once. *At the same time,* on Row 3 (3, 1, 1, 1) of 2nd rep, beg armhole shaping as foll.

Shape Armholes

Cont working yoke patt, BO 5 (6, 6, 6, 6) sts at beg of next 2 rows, then BO 4 (5, 5, 6, 7) sts at beg of next 4 (4, 6, 6, 6) rows, then BO 5 (6, 5, 6, 7) sts at beg of next 2 rows—59 sts rem for all sizes. Work Rows 1–4 of yoke patt once more, ending with a WS row.

Shape Neck + Straps

(RS) K3, p1, join new ball of yarn and BO 51 sts, p1, k3—4 sts rem each side for shoulder straps. Work each strap separately as foll.

Right Strap

Row 1 (WS) P2, k2.

Row 2 (RS) K4.

Rep Rows 1 and 2 for a total of 70 (74, 78, 84, 90) rows. Place sts on a holder.

Left Strap

Beg with a WS row, work as for right strap.

BACK

CO and work as for front until piece measures 12½ (12½, 13, 13, 13½)" (31.5 [31.5, 33, 33, 34.5] cm) from CO. Cont in rib (do not work yoke patt), working remainder of side shaping as established, until piece measures same as front to underarm, ending with a WS row.

Shape Armholes

BO 5 (6, 6, 6, 6) sts at beg of next 2 rows, then BO 4 (5, 5, 6, 7) sts at beg of next 4 (4, 6, 6, 6) rows, then BO 5 (6, 5, 6, 7) sts at beg of next 2 rows—59 sts rem for all sizes. Work Rows 1–4 of yoke patt once, ending with a WS row.

Shape Neck

(RS) K3, p1, BO 51 sts, p1, k3—4 sts rem each side.

Place sts on holders.

JOIN FRONT TO BACK

With yarn threaded on a tapestry needle and RS facing tog, sew front to back along side seams, leaving 4" (10 cm) below underarm open. Using Kitchener st (see Glossary), graft 4 sts of each front strap to corresponding 4 sts of back strap, being careful not to twist straps.

front & back

¾"
2 cm

9¼"
23.5 cm

7½ (7¾, 8, 8½, 8¾)"
19 (19.5, 20, 21.5, 22) cm

5 (5¼, 5½, 6, 6¼)"
12.5 (13.5, 14, 15, 16) cm

15¼ (17, 18¼, 19¾, 21¼)"
39.5 (43, 46.5, 50, 54) cm

15 (15, 15¾, 15¾, 16¼)"
38 (38, 40, 40, 41.5) cm

17¼ (18¾, 20, 21½, 23)"
44 (47.5, 51, 54.5, 58.5) cm

LEFT SLEEVE

With RS facing, join yarn at left front beg of strap, then pick up and knit 44 (46, 48, 52, 58) sts evenly spaced along armhole edge of strap.

Row 1 (WS) *P1, yo; rep from * to last st, p1—87 (91, 95, 103, 115) sts.

Row 2 (RS) *K1, k1 though back loop (k1tbl; this is the yo from Row 1); rep from * to last st, k1.

Rows 3–6 Work even in St st.

Row 7 P1, *p2tog; rep from * to end—44 (46, 48, 52, 58) sts rem.

Rows 8–10 Purl.

Rep these 10 rows 1 (1, 2, 2, 2) more time(s).

BO all sts.

RIGHT SLEEVE

Work as for left sleeve.

FINISHING

With yarn threaded on a tapestry needle, sew last 4" (10 cm) of side seams. Sew front side of right sleeve to front underarm, easing side into the first 2 (2, 3, 3, 3)" (5 [5, 7.5, 7.5, 7.5] cm) of underarm and leaving the remainder open. Rep for back side of sleeve. Rep for left sleeve.

Neck Edging

With crochet hook, join yarn at right back corner where back neck meets sleeve. Work 1 rnd single crochet (sc; see Glossary) evenly around entire neck opening—53 sts across back, 38 (40, 42, 46, 52) sts along left sleeve top, 53 sts across front, and 38 (40, 42, 46, 52) sts along right sleeve top. Work 1 rnd rev sc (see Glossary), working 1 st into each sc of previous row.

Weave in loose ends. Lightly steam-block entire garment, being careful not to flatten texture.

MICHELE ROSE ORNE has been designing handknits for more than twenty-five years. She is the author of *Inspired to Knit* (Interweave, 2008) and is currently entering the next phase of her career as design director for Swans Island Yarns. She lives in Camden, Maine, with her husband, four children, and various cats, dogs, bunnies, and hamsters. Visit swansislandyarns .com for a glimpse of Michele's knitting and some all-natural yarns.

Originally published in Fall 2006

glossary

ABBREVIATIONS

beg(s)	begin(s); beginning	mm	millimeter(s)	st(s)	stitch(es)
BO	bind off	M1	make one (increase)	St st	stockinette stitch
CC	contrasting color	p	purl	tbl	through back loop
cm	centimeter(s)	p1f&b	purl into front and back of same stitch	tog	together
cn	cable needle	patt(s)	pattern(s)	WS	wrong side
CO	cast on	psso	pass slipped stitch over	wyb	with yarn in back
cont	continue(s); continuing	pwise	purlwise, as if to purl	wyf	with yarn in front
dec(s)	decrease(s); decreasing	rem	remain(s); remaining	yd	yard(s)
dpn	double-pointed needles	rep	repeat(s); repeating	yo	yarnover
foll	follow(s); following	rev St st	reverse stockinette stitch	*	repeat starting point
g	gram(s)	rnd(s)	round(s)	* *	repeat all instructions between asterisks
inc(s)	increase(s); increasing	RS	right side	( )	alternate measurements and/or instructions
k	knit	sl	slip		
k1f&b	knit into the front and back of same stitch	sl st	slip st (slip 1 stitch purlwise unless otherwise indicated)	[ ]	work instructions as a group a specified number of times
kwise	knitwise, as if to knit	ssk	slip 2 stitches knitwise, one at a time, from the left needle to right needle, insert left needle tip through both front loops and knit together from this position (1 stitch decrease)		
m	marker(s)				
MC	main color				

BIND-OFFS

Three-Needle Bind-Off

Place the stitches to be joined onto two separate needles and hold the needles parallel so that the right sides of knitting face together. Insert a third needle into the first stitch on each of two needles [1] and knit them together as one stitch [2], *knit the next stitch on each needle the same way, then use the left needle tip to lift the first stitch over the second and off the needle [3]. Repeat from * until no stitches remain on first two needles. Cut yarn and pull tail through last stitch to secure.

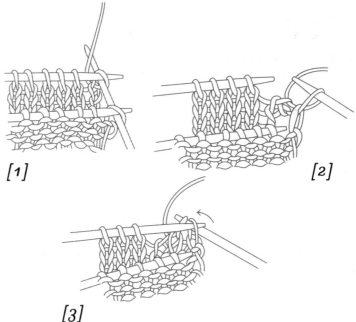

[1]

[2]

[3]

SEWN BIND-OFF

Cut yarn three times the width of the knitting to be bound off and thread onto a tapestry needle. Working from right to left, *insert tapestry needle purlwise (from right to left) through the first two stitches [1] and pull the yarn through. Bring tapestry needle knitwise (from left to right) through first stitch [2], pull yarn through, and slip this stitch off the knitting needle. Repeat from * for desired number of stitches.

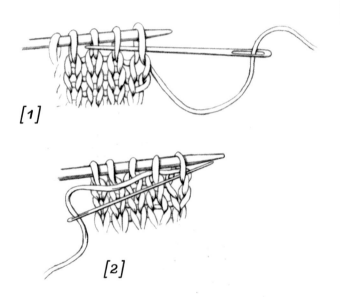

[1]

[2]

ONE-ROW BUTTONHOLE

Bring the yarn to the front of the work, slip the next stitch purlwise, then return the yarn to the back. *Slip the next stitch, pass the second stitch over the slipped stitch [1], and drop it off the needle. Repeat from * two more times. Slip the last stitch on the right needle to the left needle and turn the work around. Bring the working yarn to the back, [insert the right needle between the first and second stitches on the left needle [2], draw up a loop and place it on the left needle] four times. Turn the work around. With the yarn in back, slip the first stitch and pass the extra cast-on stitch over it [3] and off the needle to complete the buttonhole.

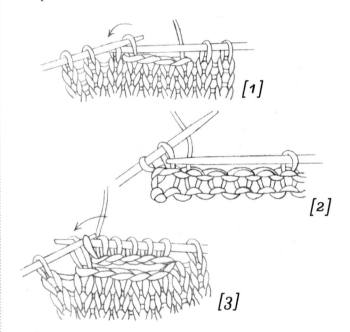

[1]

[2]

[3]

CAST-ONS

Backward-Loop Cast-On

*Loop working yarn and place it on needle backward so that it doesn't unwind. Repeat from *.

Invisible Provisional Cast-On

Make a loose slipknot of working yarn and place it on the right needle. Hold a length of contrasting waste yarn next to the slipknot and around your left thumb; hold working yarn over your left index finger. *Bring the right needle forward, then under waste yarn, over working yarn, grab a loop of working yarn and bring it forward under working yarn [1], then bring needle back behind the working yarn and grab a second loop [2]. Repeat from * for the desired number of stitches. When you're ready to work in the opposite direction, place the exposed loops on a knitting needle as you pull out the waste yarn.

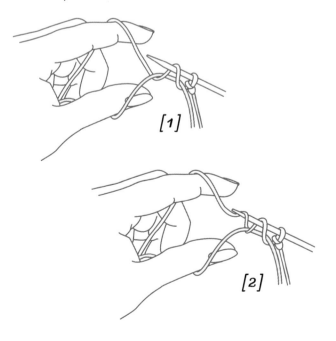

Purled Cable Cast-On

Begin by using the method of your choice to cast on two stitches onto the left needle. *Bring the working yarn around the tip of the left needle from back to front between the first two stitches on the left needle [1], wrap the yarn around the needle as if to purl, draw the yarn through [2], and place the new loop on the left needle [3]. Repeat from *, always working between the first two stitches on the needle.

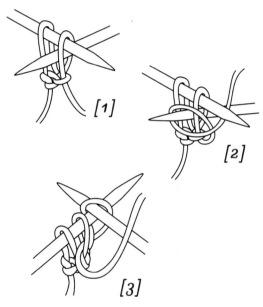

CROCHET

Crochet Chain (ch)

Make a slipknot and place it on crochet hook if there isn't a loop already on the hook. *Yarn over hook and draw through loop on hook. Repeat from * for the desired number of stitches. To fasten off, cut yarn and draw end through last loop formed.

Reverse Single Crochet

Working from left to right, insert hook into a stitch, draw through a loop, bring yarn over hook, and draw it through the first loop. *Insert hook into next stitch to the right [1], draw through a loop, bring yarn over hook again [2], and draw a loop through both loops on hook [3]. Repeat from * for the desired number of stitches.

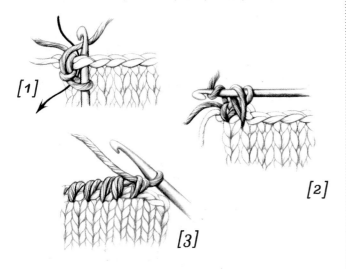

Single Crochet (sc)

*Insert hook into the second chain from the hook (or the next stitch), yarn over hook and draw through a loop, yarn over hook [1], and draw it through both loops on hook [2]. Repeat from * for the desired number of stitches.

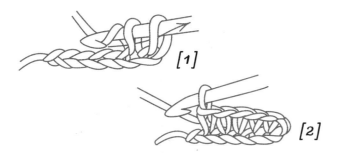

Slip-Stitch Crochet (sl st)

*Insert hook into stitch, yarn over hook and draw a loop through both the stitch and the loop already on hook. Repeat from * for the desired number of stitches.

DECREASES

Slip, Slip, Knit (ssk)

Slip two stitches individually knitwise [1], insert left needle tip into the front of these two slipped stitches, and use the right needle to knit them together through their back loops [2].

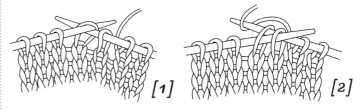

Slip, Slip, Purl (ssp)

Holding yarn in front, slip two stitches individually knitwise [1], then slip these two stitches back onto left needle (they will be twisted on the needle) and purl them together through their back loops [2].

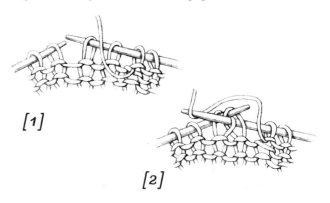

GRAFTING

Kitchener Stitch

Arrange stitches on two needles so that there is the same number of stitches on each needle. Hold the needles parallel to each other with wrong sides of the knitting together. Allowing about ½" (1.3 cm) per stitch to be grafted, thread matching yarn on a tapestry needle. Work from right to left as follows:

Step 1 Bring tapestry needle through the first stitch on the front needle as if to purl and leave the stitch on the needle *[1]*.

Step 2 Bring tapestry needle through the first stitch on the back needle as if to knit and leave that stitch on the needle *[2]*.

Step 3 Bring tapestry needle through the first front stitch as if to knit and slip this stitch off the needle, then bring tapestry needle through the next front stitch as if to purl and leave this stitch on the needle *[3]*.

Step 4 Bring tapestry needle through the first back stitch as if to purl and slip this stitch off the needle, then bring tapestry needle through the next back stitch as if to knit and leave this stitch on the needle *[4]*.

Repeat Steps 3 and 4 until one stitch remains on each needle, adjusting the tension to match the rest of the knitting as you go. To finish, bring tapestry needle through the front stitch as if to knit and slip this stitch off the needle, then bring tapestry needle through the back stitch as if to purl and slip this stitch off the needle.

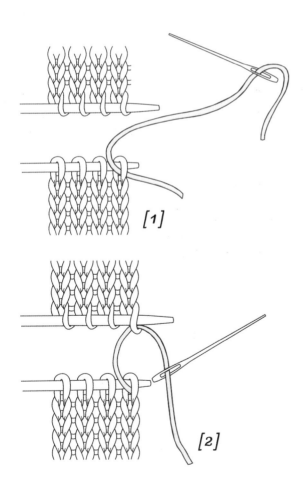

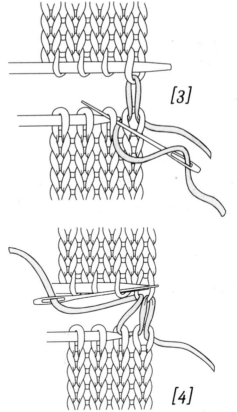

INCREASES

Bar Increase (k1f&b)

Knit into a stitch but leave it on the left needle [1], then knit through the back loop of the same stitch [2] and slip the original stitch off the needle [3].

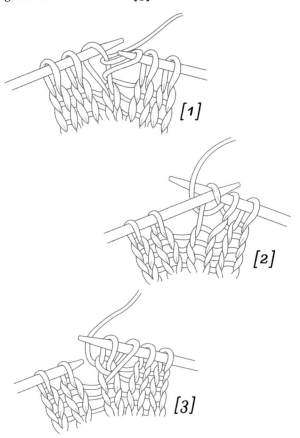

Raised Make One Increase

Note: Use the left slant if no direction of slant is specified.

LEFT SLANT (M1L)

With left needle tip, lift the strand between the last knitted stitch and the first stitch on the left needle from front to back [1], then knit the lifted loop through the back [2].

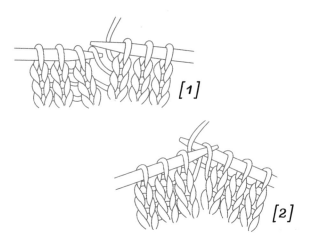

RIGHT SLANT (M1R)

With left needle tip, lift the strand between the needles from back to front [1], then knit the lifted loop through the front [2].

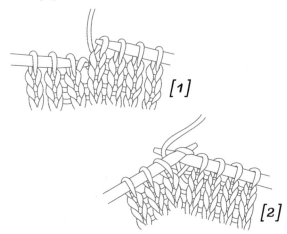

PURLWISE (M1P)

With left needle tip, lift the strand between the needles from front to back [1], then purl the lifted loop through the back [2].

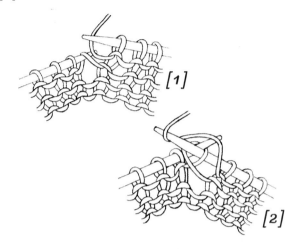

Lifted Increase

LEFT SLANT

Insert left needle tip into the back of the stitch below the stitch just knitted [1], then knit this stitch [2].

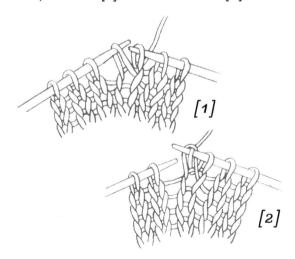

RIGHT SLANT

Knit into the back of the stitch (in the "purl bump") in the row directly below the stitch on the needle [1], then knit the stitch on the needle [2], and slip the original stitch off the needle.

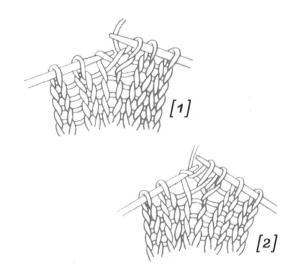

SEAMS

Mattress Stitch

Place the pieces to be seamed on a table, right sides facing up. Begin at the lower edge and work upward as follows for your stitch pattern:

STOCKINETTE STITCH WITH 1-STITCH SEAM ALLOWANCE

Insert threaded needle under one bar between the two edge stitches on one piece, then under the corresponding bar plus the bar above it on the other piece [1]. *Pick up the next two bars on the first piece [2], then the next two bars on the other [3]. Repeat from *, ending by picking up the last bar or pair of bars on the first piece.

STOCKINETTE STITCH WITH ½-STITCH SEAM ALLOWANCE

To reduce bulk in the mattress stitch seam, work as for the 1-stitch seam allowance but pick up the bars in the center of the edge stitches instead of between the last two stitches.

Garter Stitch

*Insert threaded needle under the lower purl bar between the two edge stitches on one piece [1], then the upper purl bar from the stitch next to the edge stitch on the same row of the other piece [2]. Repeat from *.

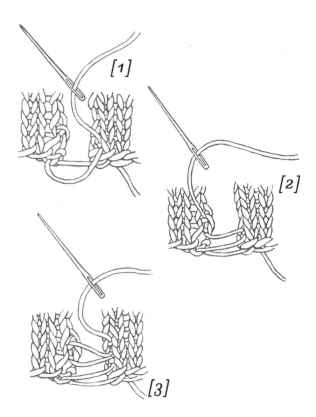

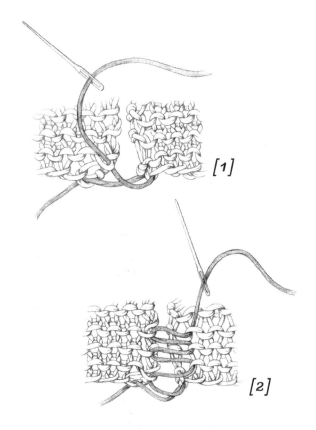

SHORT-ROWS

Short-Rows Knit Side

Work to turning point, slip next stitch purlwise [1], bring the yarn to the front, then slip the same stitch back to the left needle [2], turn the work around and bring the yarn in position for the next stitch—one stitch has been wrapped and the yarn is correctly positioned to work the next stitch. When you come to a wrapped stitch on a subsequent row, hide the wrap by working it together with the wrapped stitch as follows: Insert right needle tip under the wrap (from the front if wrapped stitch is a knit stitch; from the back if wrapped stitch is a purl stitch; [3], then into the stitch on the needle, and work the stitch and its wrap together as a single stitch.

Short-Rows Purl Side

Work to the turning point, slip the next stitch purlwise to the right needle, bring the yarn to the back of the work [1], return the slipped stitch to the left needle, bring the yarn to the front between the needles [2], and turn the work so that the knit side is facing—one stitch has been wrapped and the yarn is correctly positioned to knit the next stitch. To hide the wrap on a subsequent purl row, work to the wrapped stitch, use the tip of the right needle to pick up the wrap from the back, place it on the left needle [3], then purl it together with the wrapped stitch.

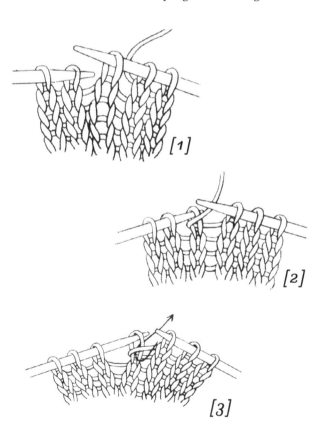

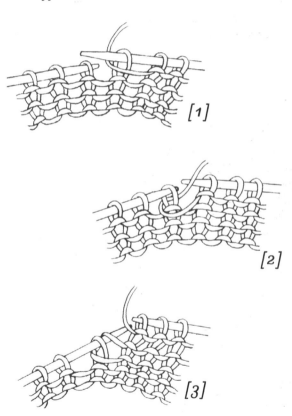

sources for yarns

Berroco Inc.
PO Box 367
14 Elmdale Rd.
Uxbridge, MA 01569
berroco.com
in Canada
S. R. Kertzer Ltd.

**Blue Moon
Fiber Arts**
56587 Mollenhour Rd.
Scappoose, OR 97056
bluemoonfiberarts.com

**Blue Sky
Alpacas**
PO Box 88
Cedar, MN 55011
blueskyalpacas.com

**Brown Sheep
Company**
100662 County Rd. 16
Mitchell, NE 69357
brownsheep.com

Cascade Yarns
PO Box 58168
1224 Andover Park E.
Tukwila, WA 98188
cascadeyarns.com

**Classic Elite
Yarns**
122 Western Ave.
Lowell, MA 01851
classiceliteyarns.com

Diamond Yarn
9697 St. Laurent,
Ste. 101
Montréal, QC
Canada H3L 2N1
and
155 Martin Ross, Unit 3
Toronto, ON
Canada M3J 2L9
diamondyarn.com

**The Fibre
Company**
Kellbourne Woolens
915 N. 28th St.
2nd Fl.
Philadelphia, PA 19130
kelbournewoolens.com

**Knitting Fever
Inc./Noro**
PO Box 336
315 Bayview Ave.
Amityville, NY 11701
knittingfever.com

**S. R. Kertzer
Ltd.**
50 Trowers Rd.
Woodbridge, ON
Canada L4L 7K6
kertzer.com

Lorna's Laces
4229 N. Honore St.
Chicago, IL 60613
lornaslaces.net

**Louet North
America**
3425 Hands Rd.
Prescott, ON
Canada K0E 1T0
louet.com

Malabrigo
malabrigoyarn.com

**Muench Yarns/
GGH**
1323 Scott St.
Petaluma, CA 94954
muenchyarns.com
in Canada
Oberlyn Yarns

Oberlyn Yarns
5640 Rue Valcourt
Brossard, QC
Canada J4W 1C5
oberlyn.ca

**Southwest
Trading
Company**
918 S. Park Ln., Ste. 102
Tempe, AZ 85281

**Tahki/Stacy
Charles Inc./
Filatura di Crosa**
70–30 80th St.,
Bldg. 36
Ridgewood, NY 11385
tahkistacycharles.com
in Canada
Diamond Yarn